Embedded Linux®

Embedded Linux®

John Lombardo

www.newriders.com

201 West 103rd Street, Indianapolis, Indiana 46290
An Imprint of Pearson Education
Boston • Indianapolis • London • Munich • New York • San Francisco

Embedded Linux®

Trademarks

Warning and Disclaimer

Publisher
David Dwyer

Associate Publisher
Al Valvano

Executive Editor
Stephanie Wall

Managing Editor
Gina Kanouse

Acquisitions Editor
Ann Quinn

Editor
Robin Drake

Product Marketing Manager
Stephanie Layton

Publicity Manager
Susan Nixon

Indexer
Chris Morris

Manufacturing Coordinator
Jim Conway

Book Designer
Louisa Klucznik

Cover Designer
Brainstorm Design, Inc.

Cover Production
Aren Howell

Proofreader
Nancy Sixsmith

Composition
Jeff Bredensteiner

❖

For Dena, Andrew, Cameron,
and Zach.

❖

Table of Contents

Introduction

About the Author

John Lombardo has been working with Linux since the "0.9" days. His ShareTheNet software product enables a novice user to easily create a highly functional router out of an old x86 computer using Linux. Lately, John has been working on several embedded Linux projects, including easy-to-use IPSec routers, ARM7-based NAT routers, and this book. John has a B.S. in computer science.

About the Technical Reviewers

These reviewers contributed their considerable hands-on expertise to the entire development process for *Embedded Linux*. As the book was being written, these dedicated professionals reviewed all the material for technical content, organization, and flow. Their feedback was critical to ensuring that *Embedded Linux* fits our reader's need for the highest-quality technical information.

Erik Andersen graduated from Brigham Young University with a B.S. in mechanical engineering and a minor in mathematics. He also completed all the course work needed for an M.S. in manufacturing engineering from BYU, but due to the arrival of his daughter Jessika, dropped out and started working for a robotics company doing workcell development, kinematics, and computer vision.

Erik started using Linux in 1994 while still an undergraduate and became a Debian developer in 1996. After buying a CD-ROM changer and finding little kernel support for such devices, Erik ended up maintaining the Linux kernel's CD-ROM subsystem from 1996 to 1998. During that time, he helped define the kernel's CD-ROM changer interface, added proper support for changers to IDE-CD, made major updates to the kernel's CD-ROM interface, ported the most useful of the old proprietary CD-ROM drivers to this new interface, and named the new interface the "Uniform CD-ROM driver."

Erik was the first Linux engineer hired by Lineo. He was team lead for developing Embedix Linux 1.0, ported the Linux (uClinux) kernel to the Atmel AT91 series CPUs (an ARM7TDMI core) and maintains the collaborative Web sites `http://opensource.lineo.com/` and `http://cvs.uclinux.org/`. Erik also maintains several pieces of widely used embedded Linux software, such as BusyBox (a suite of tiny utilities), and uClibc (a C library for embedded Linux systems).

He has been president of the Salt Lake Linux User's Group for the last two years, and lives in Salt Lake City, Utah, with his wife and two children.

Ingo Cyliax graduated from Purdue University with a degree in computer and electrical engineering and has been doing hardware and software engineering for various universities and industry as a consultant.

He works at the Indiana University Cyclotron Facility (IUCF), where he is designing particle detector electronics and data acquisition systems for detectors such as STAR. IUCF is a proton accelerator that is used for cancer treatment and radiation effects testing of electronics components. The STAR detector is at Brookhaven National Labs and is used to examine events that may have occurred under conditions shortly after the Big Bang.

In his spare time, Ingo writes articles for Circuit Cellar INK, where he hosts the "Realtime PC" column. He has also written articles on various embedded computer applications such as robot control, FPGAs genetic algorithms, and whatever else happens to strike his fancy. He also co-authored the book *Real-Time Programming: A Guide to 32-Bit Embedded Development* (Addison-Wesley, 1999, ISBN 0-201-48540-0).

Acknowledgments

A lot of work goes into writing a book. Without the following people's hard work, this book would not have been possible, so a great deal of credit must go to them for making *Embedded Linux* the book it is. However, any errors or omissions are your author's responsibility—so email me, not them.

Erik Andersen set me straight on several technical issues, including turning my bogus description of real-time into something really worth reading. Thanks also to Ingo Cyliax and Mark Whitley for providing invaluable feedback, corrections, etc.

My thanks to all of the following:

Robin Drake for guiding me through the process, providing great insight into our little part of the publishing industry.

John Keefe for testing the step-by-step procedures.

Laurie Petrycki, formerly of New Riders, for giving me the chance to write this book.

Bill Shields for pointing out Rick Lehrbaum's *Doctor Dobbs Journal* article, and for writing the hardware chapter.

Ann Quinn, my acquisitions editor, for encouraging, cajoling, and inspiring as appropriate.

I also want to thank my wife Dena and my children Andrew, Cameron, and Zachary for putting up with me for the past years while I used every nook and cranny of time to get this book out only a year late.

Finally, I want to thank my Lord and Savior, Jesus Christ.

"For by him all things were created: things in heaven and on earth, visible and invisible, whether thrones or powers or rulers or authorities; all things were created by him and for him." (Colossians 1:16)

Tell Us What You Think

As the reader of this book, you are our most important critic and commentator. We value your opinion and want to know what we're doing right, what we could do better, what areas you'd like to see us publish in, and any other words of wisdom you're willing to pass our way.

As the Executive Editor for the Web Development team at New Riders Publishing, I welcome your comments. You can fax, email, or write me directly to let me know what you did or didn't like about this book—as well as what we can do to make our books stronger.

Please note that I cannot help you with technical problems related to the topic of this book, and that due to the high volume of mail I receive, I might not be able to reply to every message.

When you write, please be sure to include this book's title and author as well as your name and phone or fax number. I will carefully review your comments and share them with the author and editors who worked on the book.

Fax: 317-581-4663
Email: Stephanie.Wall@newriders.com
Mail: Stephanie Wall
         Executive Editor
         New Riders Publishing
         201 West 103rd Street
         Indianapolis, IN 46290 USA

Introduction

You walk into your home after a long day at work. You throw your keys on the table and plop down in front of the TV. A few seconds with the remote control and your very own *I Love Lucy* marathon begins. The product that automatically records any show or subject area on TV is TiVo, and the technology behind TiVo is Linux.

We increasingly live in an automated world that George Jetson would envy. We still have computers on our desktops, but over time they'll also melt into our walls, our furniture—into the very fabric of our clothes. They'll be so easy to use that we won't have to learn how. Their operating procedure will be obvious from their physical design. At the heart of many of these devices will be the Linux operating system.

Invented by a Finnish college student named Linus Torvalds in the early 1990s, Linux has become the dominant Open Source computer operating system. Its influence has grown from its original "hacker" devotees to serious IT departments worldwide and recently to Wall Street. In fact, VA Linux's stock increased 733% in value on its first day of trading—a new record for the financial world.

Why Linux?

Why is Linux so popular? And why will it be the driving force behind the embedded computer applications that will soon sweep across the world? We'll examine several reasons in detail, but briefly these are the two most important reasons:

- **Linux is an Open Source operating system.**

  The mileage that Linux gets against other operating systems because of its Open Source nature cannot be overemphasized. The main competitor to Linux in the operating systems market is Microsoft's Windows family of products. Many other well-funded companies have brought different (and perhaps technically superior) products to market trying to compete with Windows, and for the most part those products have failed to achieve the marketplace success that their designers had hoped for. Like Windows, all of these products were proprietary. The source code to these products was closed to the public.

  The source code for Linux, on the other hand, is completely open and can be changed by anyone for any reason. You can create a product based on Linux and sell it to anyone without paying any sort of royalty. You can make any necessary changes to Linux to make your product a success in the marketplace. The only restriction is that you must share any and all changes you make to the Linux kernel with the rest of the world.

This "open source" concept really changes how computer projects—especially those at the top and bottom ends of the food chain—can be and should be designed. If you're designing a large multiuser computer system, perhaps a large Web site, and you don't consider a solution that involves Linux somewhere in the picture, you're doing yourself a disservice. Ultimately, you may not choose Linux—but you should at least consider it. The same holds true for the other end of the food chain—the very small computer systems such as embedded devices. Again, you may ultimately choose another operating system for some very good reasons, but you should consider Linux mainly because of its Open Source nature and the real benefits it brings to the table.

- **Linux has a huge percentage of mind share, which translates into lots of momentum.**

  There actually is an older, and, in some ways, technically superior Open Source operating system called *FreeBSD*. A lot of discussion has gone into why Linux has been so successful with the development community, while FreeBSD has not enjoyed the same level of recognition. Whatever the reason, Linux has gained enormous acceptance over the last few years. That acceptance has translated into mind share, which in turn has translated into momentum, which feeds back into even greater acceptance. This beneficial closed-looped cycle is driving Linux to higher and higher levels of growth and market penetration and is the main reason that Linux is so popular today and will be here for a long time to come.

What Is an Embedded System?

Okay, now we know some very specific reasons why Linux is a good choice for operating system. I'll come back to this subject in a bit more detail shortly, but first, it's important to understand exactly what constitutes an "embedded" system.

User Interface

Probably the easiest way to tell the difference between an *embedded system* and a *general-purpose computer* is the user interface. A general-purpose computer usually has a monitor, keyboard, and a mouse or other pointing device attached to it. An embedded system may not have a user interface at all, or may have a more specialized primary interface such as a single button, a touch screen, or a large control panel. Embedded systems that lack a user interface may just sit listening to a network or a sensor simply gathering data, or sending and accepting commands. You may be able to plug a monitor and keyboard into an embedded system, but this isn't the normal mode of operation. You would typically plug them in for configuration or debugging only.

Does this mean that the PCs sitting in racks at your local ISP, without monitor or keyboard, are actually embedded systems? Probably not—so it looks like we need to refine our definition a bit.

Limited Mission

The most conclusive method of determining whether a computer system fits into the "general purpose" or "embedded" category requires an examination of the system's mission in life. Embedded systems try to be cost-effective solutions to a specific problem or specification set. A general-purpose computer's mission is much like that of a Swiss Army knife. Like a Swiss Army knife, it ships from the factory with no clear mission. The Swiss Army knife can cut, saw, snip, screw, de-cork, tweeze, frappé. Similarly, the general-purpose computer can be used to process payroll, play Quake, surf the Internet, and more.

An embedded system has a limited mission. It might do 10 different things, but those 10 things are all it will ever do. For instance, the computer built into your car probably regulates fuel, gathers critical engine telemetry, and waits for a service technician's commands all at the same time, but that's all it will ever do—it doesn't matter how powerful it is, you're not going to play Quake on it.

Even though an embedded computer has a limited mission, that doesn't mean that its mission can't grow. For instance, Cisco routers can be customer-upgraded to the latest software release. Not only can bugs be fixed with the new releases, but new software can be added—expanding the usefulness of the embedded system.

Another interesting example of an embedded system's mission growing as circumstances dictate is that of NASA's Voyager 1 and 2 spacecraft (see www.jpl.nasa.gov/releases/97/vgrani97.html). Voyager 2, the first of the two spacecraft to be launched, began its journey on August 20, 1977. Voyager 1 was launched a few weeks later, on September 5, on a faster trajectory. Initially, both spacecraft were only supposed to explore two planets—Jupiter and Saturn. But the incredible success of those two first encounters and the good health of the spacecraft prompted NASA to extend Voyager 2's mission to Uranus and Neptune. As the spacecraft flew across the solar system, remote-control reprogramming gave the Voyagers greater capabilities than they possessed when they left the Earth.

> Anyone interested in embedded computers can find further fascinating reading online at NASA's Web site. Check out the chapters titled "Computers On Board Unmanned Spacecraft" in www.hq.nasa.gov/office/pao/History/computers/contents.html.

Hardware Cost/Software Complexity Ratio

We live in a time when the cost of embedded hardware components such as processors, RAM, and flash memory are falling through the floor, yet the complexity of the software required to run within embedded systems is exploding. Combined, these two trends change the rules for embedded systems engineers. Instead of simply worrying about cramming every last possible byte into a memory space stuffed full, as in years gone by, engineers must now also worry about finding time to implement all the new software features the marketplace is demanding.

This is the marketplace in which an Open Source operating system such as Linux begins to make sense. A solution based on Linux can be brought to market much more quickly than a solution that's handcrafted from a proprietary software vendor, because many more people are working on Linux than on any proprietary vendor's technology. The perception has been that these developers are hobbyist hackers who don't really know how to program, but nothing could be further from the truth. Companies such as Red Hat and VA Linux are paying a lot of money to some very bright people to make sure that the Linux OS is the best it can be.

Software Cost

The most obvious—but not necessarily most important—advantage that Linux offers is that you pay no license fee, royalties, or source license fee. In fact, you pay no fees to anyone at any time for the privilege of using Linux. This can add up to a substantial savings. Commercial embeddable operating systems like those from WindRiver and QNX can cost tens of thousands of dollars just to start development, and require royalties to be paid for each product sold.

Of course, it's important to factor into that "free" operating system the costs of developing and maintaining any changes you want to make—possibly quite long-term.

Stability

Everyone hears a lot of anecdotal evidence that Linux is very stable, especially when compared with Microsoft Windows NT. But is there any way to quantify that? Has anyone timed the frequency of the Blue Screen of Death in Windows as compared to a Linux "Oops"? The good folks at the Uptimes Project (www.uptimes.net) have done a great job trying to answer just this question. Their survey statistics showed Linux as the second most stable OS behind NetBSD and FreeBSD. As of late March 2000, the Windows NT box with the longest uptime was number 277 on the list. It had been up for 76 days. If you've ever run NT, you would agree that this is an amazing feat, but in contrast to the 575 days of the top Linux box or the 1,411 days of the top BSD box, there is really no comparison.

Portability

Linux has been ported to dozens of different architectures. The mainstream Linux source code itself is compatible with all of the following CPU architectures:

- DEC Alpha (AXP)

  www.alphalinux.org

- The ARM and StrongARM Processors

  www.arm.linux.org.uk

  www.uclinux.org

- Hitachi SuperH

  www.m17n.org/linux-sh

- IA-64

  www.linuxia64.org

- i386

- Motorola 68K series

  www.linux-m68k.org

  www.uclinux.org

- The MIPS Processor

  www.oss.sgi.com/mips/

- Motorola PowerPC

  www.linuxppc.org

- S390

  www.ibm.com

- Sparc (32 and 64 bit)

  www.ultralinux.org

Time to Market

The pace of technological innovation has been accelerating for the past 50 years, with no letup in sight. This is especially applicable in the computer field—where someone has even coined the phrase "Internet time" to describe the phenomenon.

On one hand, companies such as Intel and Motorola are creating new chipsets at a furious pace to compete with each other. On the other, hundreds of software and Internet companies are creating new protocols and ways of hooking computers to humans and to each other. This puts a lot of pressure on embedded OS companies such as QNX and WindRiver. They must support the hardware technologies as they first come out or soon after; then they must support those technologies long-term. The real problem for the embedded OS companies, however, is software support. They must constantly play catchup on the software front. Many of the newest software technologies are being developed using Linux, so by definition the technology is available there first. Technologies that are not developed on Linux are usually created on Microsoft Windows. Because of Linux's huge development base, the important technologies developed on Windows are quickly migrated to Linux.

One more reason that Linux speeds time to market is that you can often use the same OS for the development host as you would for the target host.

Open Source

Except for cost, all of the reasons previously outlined are technical issues. For instance, Linux is very stable, but so are the commercial embedded OS choices. The one area that really sets Linux apart is the fact that it's Open Source. This fact, above all technical issues, should make Linux (or perhaps some other Open Source operating system) the OS of choice until eliminated for some specific reason.

So what does it mean to be Open Source?

Version 1.7 of the Open Source Definition (www.opensource.com)
Free Redistribution

The license may not restrict any party from selling or giving away the software as a component of an aggregate software distribution containing programs from several different sources. The license may not require a royalty or other fee for such sale.

Source Code

The program must include source code, and must allow distribution in source code as well as compiled form. Where some form of a product is not distributed with source code, there must be a well-publicized means of obtaining the source code for no more than a reasonable reproduction cost—preferably, downloading via the Internet without charge. The source code must be the preferred form in which a programmer would modify the program. Deliberately obfuscated source code is not allowed. Intermediate forms such as the output of a preprocessor or translator are not allowed.

Derived Works

The license must allow modifications and derived works, and must allow them to be distributed under the same terms as the license of the original software.

Integrity of the Author's Source Code

The license may restrict source code from being distributed in modified form only if the license allows the distribution of "patch files" with the source code for the purpose of modifying the program at build time. The license must explicitly permit distribution of software built from modified source code. The license may require derived works to carry a different name or version number from the original software.

No Discrimination Against Persons or Groups

The license must not discriminate against any person or group of persons.

No Discrimination Against Fields of Endeavor

The license must not restrict anyone from making use of the program in a specific field of endeavor. For example, it may not restrict the program from being used in a business, or from being used for genetic research.

Distribution of License

The rights attached to the program must apply to all to whom the program is redistributed without the need for execution of an additional license by those parties.

License Must Not Be Specific to a Product

The rights attached to the program must not depend on the program's being part of a particular software distribution. If the program is extracted from that distribution and used or distributed within the terms of the program's license, all parties to whom the program is redistributed should have the same rights as those that are granted in conjunction with the original software distribution.

License Must Not Contaminate Other Software

The license must not place restrictions on other software that is distributed along with the licensed software. For example, the license must not insist that all other programs distributed on the same medium must be Open Source software.

Advantages of Open Source

- **You can find any bug when you have the source.**

  For developers, nothing is more frustrating than running into a wall when debugging code, or worse, when trying to debug a customer's problem. Running into a wall means tracing your code all the way to a piece of code to which you don't have the source and into which you therefore can't trace, and the software fails in that code. Sometimes, the problem is in the code to which you don't have the source, but many times it's in your own code—perhaps you're not correctly using the code for which you don't have the source. It doesn't matter—without the source, you can spend hours or even days staring at your code, and never find the problem. If you had the source code to the function you're calling, you might quickly see what the problem is and resolve it within minutes. Or perhaps there really is a bug in the code you're calling—you can fix it or have the maintainer fix it and get on with your work.

Many developers have resigned themselves to not seeing the source code to some of the software they're using; they believe that these walls are just a fact of life in their chosen profession. It's simply not true. Open Source developers who are smart enough to be able to dig deeper to the next level of code (all the way to the kernel, if necessary) simply don't run into walls and can debug any software problem. Indeed, any problem that just can't be solved by debugging is almost certainly a hardware problem.

- **You can get other people (experts) to fix code for you.**

In 1999, I worked on a software application project whose users had a lot of experience with the application but none with Linux. We had to create a complete package, including a custom installation emphasizing a hardware set that our installed base of customers already had.

Several weeks into the beta cycle, a customer found a problem with a system board. Not only were we able to debug the problem all the way to the driver level, but we proposed a fix to the maintainer of the driver. He found that while this particular fix would work for our unique circumstances, a better fix was possible that would handle a whole class of problems. He implemented that fix and gave me the source code to the new driver. Had we not been working on an Open Source operating system, we would not have been able to find the problem and make a fix ourselves. Had the problem been with the driver for a generic piece of hardware for a large closed-source operating system, we would have had a difficult time getting the attention we needed and the problem might still be there.

- **You can find out how things are supposed to work.**

Having the source code to all the drivers in Linux makes writing drivers much easier. If the code writer needs a specific feature, he or she can just look at how other drivers implement that feature. In fact, the first step when writing a new driver is usually finding a driver similar to the one you need, copying it, and then modifying the new copy for your situation.

- **Good documentation is available.**

Some Open Source software packages are not well documented. Linux, on the other hand, is very well documented. Many free documents are available from the Linux Documentation Project, and dozens of books are available for purchase. Of course, the ultimate authority on how a software package works— the source code itself—is available for any Open Source software product.

Disadvantages of Open Source

- **It's more difficult to protect intellectual property.**

  There are many market reasons for which you might not want to release your intellectual property: You want to get or keep ahead of the competition, you don't own all the code your IP is based on, and so on. If you have intellectual property that you're not planning to share with the rest of the world, you need to be very careful to not include any source code from other Open Source projects, even if you might have otherwise reduced your time to market. Including source code from (or basing your software on) other Open Source projects will generally cause your source code to be covered by the terms of that Open Source project—a bad thing for those wanting to maintain intellectual property.

  For application code, there are many closed-source apps under Linux (the most notable being Netscape). In kernel space, there are many examples of binary-only kernel modules (such as DiskOnChip, used in later examples in this book). In kernel space, though, the maintenance burden is often a very high price to pay. Since the kernel has many options that change the module interface (such as SMP versus UP, large memory model versus small, and so on), even a single kernel release may require several builds for every platform. Furthermore, kernel interfaces change, leaving the proprietor of the binary-only kernel with broken code in need of constant repair. Also, when a bug crops up, the standard set of kernel developers may refuse to help those using binary-only kernel modules and instead refer them to the modules' proprietor.

- **Kernel releases come fast and furious.**

  Linux kernel changes can come out very quickly and can differ significantly from release to release. If you feel you must run on the latest version, this can be quite demanding.

- **Kernel releases don't always appear when expected.**

  This can be difficult if you want to plan a release of your product based on a feature set available in the newest kernel, but don't want to release beta code.

- **It's difficult to know whether your changes will be incorporated.**

  If you make changes to the kernel, you can't be sure that they'll be incorporated into the mainline source code. Sometimes a kernel change that works perfectly is completely rejected by the kernel maintainers as being philosophically wrong for Linux. (You want them to be incorporated so that other people can do the maintenance on these changes for you when kernel interfaces change.)

- **Linux is not afraid of breaking backward compatibility.**

  Unlike other operating systems, Linux is not full of "cruft." That is, it doesn't have a lot of version-specific code. This makes reading the source code much easier because it's not littered with a lot of #ifdefs and other compatibility code. Unfortunately, this means that sometimes programs that used to run just fine under Linux may stop running with newer kernels. It's usually up to the driver maintainer to make sure that the driver is kept up to date, so you may spend time fixing bugs where there were none earlier, because an interface changed or a service simply went away.

How the GNU Affects You

The two most important licenses you must understand if you intend to use Linux in your development project are the *GNU General Public License (GPL)* and the *GNU Lesser General Public License (LGPL)*. The source code to the Linux operating system is copyrighted under the GPL, and the GNU C Library is covered under the LGPL. See Appendixes A and B for the full texts of these licenses.

How the GPL and LGPL Are Similar

Since both the GPL and LGPL are creations of the Free Software Foundation, they're very similar. They both have the following important attributes:

- **Copyleft**

  The term *copyleft*, invented by the folks at the GNU project, is a pun on the word *copyright*. Copyleft refers to the clauses of an Open Source license that stop an individual or corporation from taking a copy of source code that's under GPL license, making modifications, changing the license, and thereby "closing" their modified—and presumably better—version of the original source code. Once a piece of source code is placed under the GPL or LGPL, the code itself and all derivations of it are forever available in source form to any interested party. Should a third party make changes to this source code and then distribute it, they are required to make both their changes and the original source code available to anyone they distribute the software to.

- **Availability**

  If you make modifications to source code under GPL, your best bet is to get those changes folded back into the standard source set by submitting a patch to the code's maintainer. You can usually figure out who the maintainer is by looking for a README file in the root directory of the source tar file. If your changes are accepted by the maintainer, then you're relieved of a couple of burdens.

First, you don't have to keep reapplying (and fixing) your patch when a new version of the code appears. This can become quite tiresome, especially if the code is released often and you want to keep up to date.

Second, the GPL requires that you accompany your product with either the source to the changes or a written offer of the source code valid for at least three years. It's generally accepted that if your changes are available in a standard distribution, you can simply point people who want those changes to that standard distribution.

Both version 2 of the GNU General Public License and the GNU Lesser General Public License are reproduced in this book's appendixes. If you're considering using Linux as the operating system for your embedded application, you should take the time to read and understand these licenses. Unlike a lot of legal language, they're quite readable and understandable from a software developer's point of view.

How the GPL and LGPL Are Different

Licensing source code under the GPL or the LGPL produces similar results. Any changes to either code set must be made available to anyone interested, and so on. The only real difference is whether proprietary code can link with the Open Source code. The LGPL allows an entity to link its proprietary code to the Open Source code and distribute resultant binaries with no restrictions, as long as those binaries are dynamically linked. Binaries are still covered under whatever proprietary license the owner wants.

The most obvious example is the GNU C library, glibc. Since it's released under the LGPL, a proprietary software company such as Oracle can compile and link its database application in-house, put the binaries on a CD, and ship those binaries only. Those binaries will run under the Linux kernel, which is covered by the GPL, using the dynamic glibc C libraries, which are covered under the LGPL. If Oracle decided to make changes to the C library or the Linux operating system, they would have to make those changes available to whoever wanted them, but they wouldn't have to make the database itself public because it's dynamically linked with the LGPL glibc.

If your entire embedded application environment is really short on space, and the entire application lives within a single executable, you may want to link it statically. If you do that and you use a library under LGPL, such as the glibc library, you'll have to make object code or source code available to all your customers. Section 6c of the LGPL allows you to make a written offer of the object code, if you prefer. Therefore, statically linking your code can become a maintenance, support, and liability nightmare for embedded device manufacturers. I suggest dynamically linking your code so you don't fall into this trap.

When Is Linux Inappropriate?

Which brings us to the topic of when Linux is inappropriate. Clearly, no operating system is perfect for all situations. Because Linux carries very little baggage, it covers more situations than most—but it's not perfect for everything. You should consider the following points carefully before deciding to use Linux as the operating system for your embedded application.

- **You may not be able to live with the GPL.**

  Probably the thing that should concern an embedded developer the most is the GPL and LGPL licenses. These Open Source licenses are *good* things; without them, we wouldn't even have the choice of using Linux in embedded applications—the huge growth of embedded applications would instead be much slower and limited to proprietary software. However, these licenses make it impossible to bring to market some applications based on Linux.

- **Linux is *big*.**

  Another area of concern for anyone looking at Linux as an embedded application operating system is its size. Even when you pull everything you can out of the OS, it's still pretty big. If you're building a nano-probe the size of an ant and have 100 bytes of memory to do everything, Linux is not for you. Compressed, Linux takes about 400KB. When it's uncompressed at boot time, it's going to take almost one megabyte. (Although uClinux can run the kernel plus a few basic user space apps in about 800KB.) For a real embedded application, the smallest realistic memory size is probably around 2MB.

- **Suitability.**

  There are some embedded applications for which other operating systems are just better suited. For instance, if you're building a handheld PIM, it would be a lot of work to beat PalmOS in terms of functionality and size. Instead of concentrating on your application, you would have to concentrate on making the pen work, small memory management, and so on.

- **Security.**

  The debate rages on as to whether an Open Source operating system is more secure than one whose source is closed. On one hand, a bad guy who doesn't have access to the source for your embedded application can't stare at that source code for days trying to figure out an approach with which to attack your device. This bad guy is restricted to trying random attacks until he finds one that works, or finding general vulnerabilities in the OS you chose.

On the other hand, if the bad guy can figure out which version of Linux you're using, he can get the source code and look for vulnerabilities. The question is, will he find one? Open Source software is considered by many to be more secure because many more eyes are looking at the code and fixing security problems.

Each argument has its merits. The bottom line is this: If you use Linux and your embedded application holds valuable data on a network, you should make sure that you can distribute security updates to your customers. Security problems will be found, and if you can't upgrade the software on your embedded application, you'll have problems.

- Market pressures.

Of course, a vast array of nontechnical issues may require you to choose another operating system for your embedded application. Perhaps your customer or the market in general demands a particular operating system. Perhaps the investor community will pour money into your little startup if you use OS Brand X instead of Linux.

The Embedded Linux Workshop

In the pages of this book, I'll specify the hardware for and give you the software to create your own working embedded Linux appliance. It comes complete with all the software and scripts necessary to get the machine up and working on a network—all you have to do is add the application.

Several embedded Linux development groups exist these days; all of them have some great ideas. The Embedded Linux Workshop in Chapter 7 is the minimum software necessary to embed your application. There's no great learning curve; it's all right there, very simple and easy to understand.

The feature set that the Embedded Linux Workshop gives you is complete enough to get you started:

- It uses a floppy disk, hard drive, or flash to boot the Linux kernel and a small initrd file system.

- It doesn't require a keyboard or monitor for production. However, you can attach them for use with an optional debugging package.

- It brings up a network connection.

- It has an easy-to-follow procedure for adding optional packages. This way, your software doesn't have to mingle with the Workshop's source tree.

- It has a Web-based administration package so that you can administer your appliance over the network.

- The entire Embedded Linux Workshop is covered under the GPL.

Conventions Used in This Book

The following conventions are used in this book:

Convention	Usage
italic	New terms being defined.
`monospace text`	Commands, syntax lines, and so on, as well as Internet addresses such as `www.LinuxDevices.com`.
➡	Code-continuation characters are inserted into code when a line shouldn't be broken, but we simply ran out of room on the page.

I

Software

Software Considerations

YOU KNOW YOU WANT TO BUILD AN EMBEDDED APPLICATION, and you know you want to use Linux as the operating system. Where do you start?

With the hardware.

The hardware choices you make—processor, memory, flash, and so on—drive what you will do with the software. Because no software license cost is associated with Linux, most of your cost will be in the hardware itself. The more units you sell, the more true that is. Therefore, in any high-volume application, it's important to get the hardware right before you ever worry about the software. Linux has been adapted to many different microprocessors and microcontrollers, and more are supported all the time. Chances are that Linux already supports the processor you'll choose in some way. If not, and you have the time and expertise, you can support it yourself.

After you select the hardware you want to use, it's time to see how well Linux supports that hardware. So fire up your browser and search the Internet for Web sites devoted to `Linux + your hardware device`. Here are some good places:

- www.google.com
- www.LinuxDevices.com
- www.LinuxHardware.net
- www.LinHardware.com

After you've finally decided on your hardware platform, it's time to nail down exactly what you want the software to do. This chapter presents several software-related issues you'll need to consider.

Note: If you want to support a soft modem (also known as *winmodems*), you can write the driver for Linux and install it as a module at boot time. Linus doesn't like this, but admits that it doesn't violate the GPL.

Embedded Linux Toolkits

Porting Linux to a new hardware platform can be a daunting task. Fortunately, several embedded Linux toolkits are designed to simplify the job of building the binary that runs your device. Some toolkits, such as Lineo's Embedix and Monte Vista's Hard Hat Linux, are broadly focused, and are able to work on many processors for lots of different applications. Others are from smaller companies and focus on narrower processor sets and more limited application ranges. Still others, such as PeeWeeLinux, are not products distributed by companies, but rather projects built by a set of like-minded hackers in the traditional Open Source model.

Here are a few things to consider when you're looking for an embedded Linux toolkit:

- **Hardware support.** Does the Linux toolkit include support for the processor you want to use? If the toolkit doesn't already support that processor, does the toolkit vendor have the ability to develop that support quickly enough for your purposes? If so, how much will it cost? Does it fit in your budget?

- **Documentation.** Is the toolkit well documented? Are all of the programs involved documented? Does the documentation cover both high-level concepts such as architecture white papers and low-level documentation such as how to build binaries, how to add your software to the code base, and reference manuals to the build and runtime software?

- **Adaptability.** How adaptable is the embedded Linux toolkit to the particular application you're going to use? If it's a very narrow toolkit and you'll use it for several projects, how much work will be involved in changing the toolkit to the projects for which it's not as well suited?

- **Developer support.** What kind of developer support does the toolkit company offer, and how expensive is it? If you need a bug fixed, a question answered, or a device driver written, how quickly can you get a response from the company? Is a listserv available for the users of the product? If one is available, how active is it? Is anyone from the company answering questions on the list?

- **Field upgradeability.** Are facilities available in the toolkit for upgrading the software in the field? Does the toolkit company offer any means for delivering those upgrades, or is that left to you?

- **User interface.** If your application requires some sort of user interface, what are your options? Does the embedded Linux toolkit offer some sort of embedded video interface? If so, how much room does it take? If not, is there some sort of Web-based interface available for configuration?

  Note that the toolkit itself may not have any support for a graphical interface. Several Open Source projects and several commercial products are aimed at building small-footprint graphical user interfaces. For more information, see `http://www.linuxdevices.com/articles/AT9202043619.html`.

- **Track record.** Does the toolkit vendor have any examples of customers who have created a similar product out in the field? How successful was that vendor with the toolkit?

Kernel Features

The Linux kernel runs on a vast array of hardware architectures—everything from handhelds to mainframes. To support this sort of scalability, the kernel is highly configurable.

There are several ways of configuring the kernel (note that I'm using the word *configure* quite loosely here):

- Typing `make config`, `make menuconfig`, or `make xconfig` in the root of the kernel source runs the standard kernel configure routines. You can turn options on or off or sometimes compile them as modules so they can be loaded at runtime.

- There are hundreds—perhaps even thousands—of kernel patches floating around the Internet. Some are very small—enough to fix a small bug in one file. Medium-size patches may affect a half-dozen files and add support for a particular hardware device. Some large patches add or affect many dozens of files and add support for new architectures. Often applying a patch adds new questions or entire screens to the kernel-configuration screens previously described.

- The One True Method of really "configuring" the kernel to do exactly what you want is to hack on it yourself. Until recently, this was an exercise only for those who have lots of time and patience—the Linux kernel source code is well structured but somewhat obtuse. Linus doesn't believe in cluttering up the source with comments for the uninitiated (see Chapter 5 of Documentation/Coding Style in the Linux source tree).

Fortunately, times have changed and there are now several good overviews of the Linux kernel. Perhaps the most lucid is *Understanding the Linux Kernel* by Daniel Pierre Bovet and Marco Cesati (O'Reilly, 2000).

Networking, Filesystems, and Executable Formats

Some embedded Linux applications have no use for the networking code. Be sure to configure the kernel so that the networking code is skipped if you don't need it; it takes up a lot of space. Also, make sure that your kernel supports only the one or two filesystem types you actually need. Finally, you probably need only one executable format, ELF (Executable and Linking Format), for your embedded application, so be sure to turn off all the rest. For details on the ELF file format, consult the following documents:

- http://ibiblio.org/pub/Linux/GCC/ELF.doc.tar.gz
- http://ibiblio.org/pub/Linux/GCC/elf.ps.gz

In general, it's a good idea to look through the documentation for all the choices in the kernel build menu. If you're using make menuconfig to configure the kernel, you can press the question mark (?) at any time to get information on the choice you have highlighted.

While you're developing your embedded device, it's handy to enable loadable module support in the kernel. That way, if you need support for a feature that you hadn't anticipated, you can go back, recompile the modules you need, copy them onto your device, and load them. Without loadable module support, you have to recompile the whole kernel, which can be a bit of a pain. When you're done developing the device, you can save some amount of RAM and ROM space by recompiling the kernel without loadable module support and with your drivers compiled directly into the kernel. However, you should figure out exactly how much of a savings this is and whether it's worth it—having loadable module support may be useful for upgrading drivers in the field.

Execute-in-Place (XIP)

One way you may be able to save a lot of RAM requirements is to run your executable programs directly from the long-term storage (ROM or flash) where they reside. This is called *execute-in-place* (or *XIP* for short).

On a desktop system, your application lives on the hard disk and must be read into RAM for execution. However, most embedded applications don't have a hard drive for long-term storage; instead, they have some sort of memory device, such as ROM or flash. Unlike a hard drive, these memory devices may be directly addressable by the CPU, like RAM. You can use the direct addressability of these memory devices to reduce your RAM requirements. Instead of copying the executable code from the memory device into RAM, an XIP system sets up the kernel structures that normally point into the RAM copy directly at the long-term storage locations. The code executes just as it would if it were copied to RAM. Depending on the speed of the processor, memory, and flash, there could be a performance penalty for using XIP.

Figure 1.1 shows the difference between normal execution and execution in place (XIP):

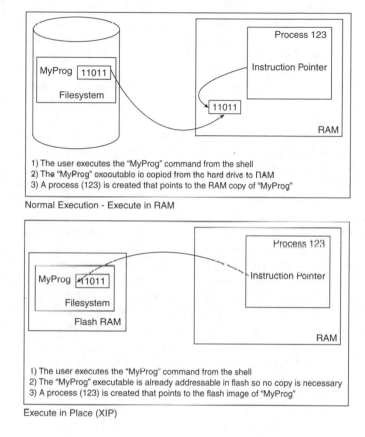

1) The user executes the "MyProg" command from the shell
2) The "MyProg" executable is copied from the hard drive to RAM
3) A process (123) is created that points to the RAM copy of "MyProg"

Normal Execution - Execute in RAM

1) The user executes the "MyProg" command from the shell
2) The "MyProg" executable is already addressable in flash so no copy is necessary
3) A process (123) is created that points to the flash image of "MyProg"

Execute in Place (XIP)

Figure 1.1   XIP illustration.

Real-Time Operating Systems

Most of the time, it's not very important exactly how long a specific task takes to complete on a computer. For instance, when someone hits a key on the keyboard, they expect a letter to appear "instantly"—but how fast is "instantly"? It could be anywhere from a few tens of milliseconds to a couple of hundred milliseconds. You're probably not going to notice the difference between any two timings under 50 milliseconds (about 1/20th of a second). However, the timing of some operations in some computer applications is crucial. For instance, if your application moves a robotic arm to a precise location so that it can pick up a chip from a stack, then to another location so it can lay down the chip at a precise location on a PC board, the timing of the movement operations must be exact. This is when you need a real-time OS.

For instance, most modern cars have antilock braking systems. In these systems, special sensors detect when one or more wheels begin to "lock up"—a dangerous situation that can cause the vehicle (and its occupants!) to slide. In these situations, it's imperative that when the sensors detect a wheel beginning to lock, the braking on that wheel be reduced immediately. Have you ever worked on a computer system where you started a new program and the entire computer became unresponsive for several seconds? Imagine what would happen if the computer controlling your antilock brakes was similarly busy and unresponsive—right when a deer jumped in front of your car! This is a situation where you need what's called *hard real time*.

A hard real-time OS guarantees that, without fail, no matter what else happens, a response to an event will occur within a specified fixed time. For example, when wheel lockup is detected, braking for that wheel must be reduced within a certain number of milliseconds. In this example, a hard limit exists on how long the system can take to respond to the wheel lockup condition. This hard limit means that this is a hard real-time task—first, because there's an absolute limit on the amount of time available for a response, and second, because bad things will happen if the system fails to respond within the specified time limit. These two features of the task to be performed make it clear that the task requires a hard real-time operating system.

When working with a *soft* real-time OS, on the other hand, when an event occurs the system will try its best to service the event within an average response time. For example, when playing a game of Quake III, when a player fires a rocket at another player there's an expectation that the game program will draw a fiery explosion onscreen, make explosion noises, and dutifully subtract health from your opponent. With all of this complexity added to the existing events in the game, it's very likely that the frame rate of the game may drop slightly while rendering the explosion and playing back the additional audio, since these tasks require additional CPU time. If the frame rate should drop from 50 frames per second (fps) to, say, 40 fps for the duration of the explosion, no harm is done—the player continues to enjoy her game, since the system is still "fast enough." Being "fast enough" is a defining characteristic of soft real-time systems. In this case, no fixed frame rate is required of the system, and no harm occurs should the frame rate decrease slightly.

Both hard and soft real-time systems are useful, but they have distinctly different uses. In fact, a hard real-time OS usually accommodates tasks requiring both hard and soft real-time response.

Several attributes differentiate a real-time operating system from a standard operating system, as shown in the following list.

- **Response time predictability.** A hard real-time OS guarantees that the timing of some operations will be precise within its stated limitations. These response times are much faster than those of a typical operating system—they're measured in tens of microseconds (millionths of a second) instead of milliseconds (thousandths of a second).

- **Schedulability.** In a hard real-time operating system, a process can be scheduled to perform at a very precise time in the future or at a very precise interval. Again, the precision is down to the microsecond level instead of the millisecond level.

- **Stability under pressure.** In a hard real-time system, the processor can become inundated with far more signals from different sources than it can handle; however, some of those signals are much more important than other signals and must be recognized and dealt with. The ability to prioritize a vast array of different signals quickly and efficiently is another hallmark of a good real-time system.

For more details on embedded real-time systems, see Raj Rajkumar, et al, *The Concise Handbook of Linux for Embedded Real-Time Systems Version 1.0* (Pittsburgh, Pennsylvania: TimeSys Corporation, 2000), p. 5. In addition, `www.RealTimeLinux.org` provides a lot of information about real-time Linux.

Several real-time Linux kernel projects are underway, as shown in Table 1.1.

Table 1.1   Real-Time Linux Projects

Address	Title	Site Sponsor
`www.rtlinux.org`	RTLinux—Real time Linux	New Mexico Institute of Technology
`http://server.aero. polimi.it/projects/rtai/`	RTAI—Real Time Application Interface	Dipartimento di Ingegneria Aerospaziale Politecnico di Milano
`www.ittc.ukans.edu/kurt/`	KURT—The KU Real Time Linux	University of Kansas
`http://linux.ece.uci.edu/ RED-Linux/index.html`	RED-Linux	University of California, Irvine

Creating or Acquiring a Development Environment

Before you can even start coding, you must either create or acquire a development environment for your chosen microprocessor or microcontroller. You'll need a C compiler, assembler (part of the compiler), linker, runtime library, debugging tools, and perhaps an emulator. The fastest way to acquire a development environment is to get it from one of the embedded Linux toolkits. Usually this is free or a nominal price.

Booting the Kernel

How the computer loads the operating system into memory and starts it is an issue that most software developers never have to think about. Most of us work on PCs or similar platforms that have a BIOS that does the dirty work of setting up the computer's hardware and finding and loading the OS loader (for example, LILO or GRUB) into RAM so that the kernel can start. The most we ever have to think about is which OS loader to use and how to configure it properly.

Welcome to the world of embedded devices, where you may start with a manual that says only something like this:

> "Hard Reset (HRESET)—Input" causes the hard reset exception to be taken and the physical address of the handler is always x'FFF00100'.
>
> *PowerPC 601 RISC Microprocessor User's Manual* (IBM Corporation, 1993), p. 5-16.

It's now up to *you* to write the assembly code to do the following:

1. Initialize all of the hardware.
2. Move the OS loader into memory from storage (or perhaps you just load the OS itself).
3. Jump into the code you just loaded.

Fortunately, most development boards for the various microcontrollers and microprocessors come with ample documentation and sample code for startup. There are also many examples on the Internet for the many different processors that Linux supports.

Software Size

Unlike a general-purpose computer system, an embedded system only requires enough software to actually get a specific set of jobs done. This means you can do without a lot of the fluff that normally goes into a general-purpose computer system such as X windows, email and newsreaders, games, and so on. By doing this, you can make the software image much smaller. This is important because you normally don't have a hard drive in an embedded application. Even when you do have one for storage, it may be better to put the system software and applications in ROM or flash so they aren't as vulnerable to corruption. Both ROM and flash are much more expensive byte-for-byte than space on a hard drive, so it's important to include just the software that your embedded application actually uses.

Another reason to limit the software that ships in your embedded application is simple; if it's not there, it can't break. It's usually very inconvenient to upgrade the software in an embedded application—sometimes it's impossible.

However, a tradeoff exists between engineering time and footprint size. Generally, the longer you engineer the product, the smaller and more efficient you can make it, reducing your memory requirements, and thus reducing the cost of each unit. However, the more time you spend on efficiency, the fewer features the product will have, given constant engineering resources. Also, if the product sits in engineering too long, you may lose considerable market advantage to your competitors.

Reducing the Software Footprint

So how do you reduce the memory/storage requirements of your embedded Linux application? Generally, there are three ways:

- Include only the software you need.
- Compile the software to reduce size.
- Compress the resulting software.

Chapter 2, "Minimal Linux," details how to reduce the size of your embedded Linux application.

Upgrading the Software in Place

Most software systems must be upgraded at some point in their lifetime for a variety of reasons: bugs and security vulnerabilities are found and fixed, new features are required, and so on. Embedded applications are no exception. However, if upgradeability is not designed in from the beginning, the upgrade process will be difficult or even impossible. For instance, unless you want your customers to do minor surgery on your embedded device, you shouldn't ship the software in ROM. The only way to replace software that's burned into ROM is to replace the ROM chip. Also, if you only have enough memory-plus-storage in the device to actually run the application, upgrading is very dangerous because there's no good place to put the software. You can download the new code over the old code, but one small error and your customer now owns a doorstop instead of an embedded Linux application.

So how do you design your upgrade process from the beginning?

1. Start by putting only the most low-level code in ROM and putting the rest in flash. The code that's in ROM will probably never be replaced, so you have to get it right. You may want to put the upgrade code itself in ROM; that way, no matter what happens in the field, the user can "upgrade" to a working set of code even after messing up an upgrade attempt.

2. Configure the machine with enough storage or RAM to hold two complete copies of the software in the machine simultaneously. Unless you put the upgrade software in ROM as described above, your application will become a doorstop if a catastrophic event occurs, such as loss of power. You want to reduce this "doorstop time" to the minimum possible. For instance, if your application

downloads the new software directly on top of the old software and this process takes 20 seconds, you have a doorstop time of 20 seconds. If the customer's power is lost, a cable is kicked loose, or the cat jumps onto the keyboard any time during this 20 seconds, your customer now has a doorstop—plus, they're angry, and it will cost you money.

Now imagine that you have $2^{1/2}$ times the amount of flash that you really need in the device (the extra $1/2$ is for growth). Instead of overwriting the old code with the new, you store it in the extra room in the flash as it's downloading. When all the code is safely written to flash, you then change a few pointers to complete the update. Now your "doorstop time" is just a few milliseconds, while the pointers are updated in flash.

This procedure has other advantages. After all the new software has come across, you can make sure that the binary image is intact by including some checksum code. You can also make sure that the user has downloaded the right thing and has a later version than the one currently installed. None of this is possible if you overwrite the current software with the new as the download occurs.

3. Put all of the configuration information for your machine in a single place, such as a single file in flash. This makes all your software much easier to manage. It makes the upgrade process easier because there's only one file to manage (and perhaps change) during the upgrade process. Remember that you may have several versions out in the field, however, and you don't want to force users to move from a very old version to the newest version by upgrading through each version in between. If your software changes a lot between releases, the permutations can become enormous quickly, so keeping things as simple as possible helps the user avoid losing configuration information.

Of course, there are many ways to accomplish this objective. The process described above is more costly on a per-unit basis than simply putting everything in flash memory. Depending on your application and economies, it may make more sense to put everything in flash—just realize that in some instances you could end up with a lot of doorstops out in the field.

2

Minimal Linux

WHEN BUILDING AN EMBEDDED APPLICATION, the primary concern is almost always the size of the distribution and how much memory it will take. The device you're building is usually much smaller physically than a general-purpose computer, and it usually has less memory and storage. Therefore, the embedded software must be much more efficient than software that runs on a general-purpose computer. Fortunately, a lot of research has been done to optimize software for storage and memory usage—because they were so much more expensive in years gone by.

This chapter explores some of the various ways to make a running Linux system as small as possible, and looks at the different methods available to the developer of an embedded appliance.

Before we delve into optimizing for size, we should take a look at how a typical Linux system works, and some interesting alternatives to the typical system.

A typical desktop Linux system has three major software layers—the Linux kernel, a C library, and application code (see Figure 2.1):

- The kernel has sole and complete control over the hardware. Its drivers talk with the hardware on behalf of applications.

- The next layer up from the kernel is the C library in a typical Linux system. Among other things, the C library translates POSIX API calls into a form that the kernel likes, and then calls the kernel, passing the parameters from the application code to the kernel.

- Finally, farthest out from the hardware is the application code. The applications cause the Linux kernel (and thus the hardware—whether it's a router, a personal organizer, or a camera) to perform the intended task.

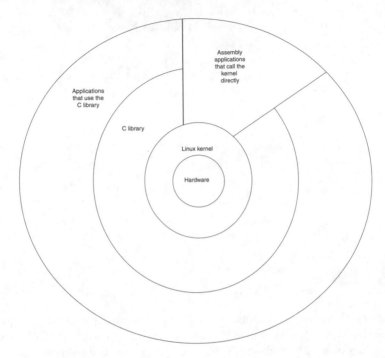

Figure 2.1   Layers in a typical desktop Linux system.

When designing your embedded application, it's important to realize that you can break this hierarchy. For example, your applications don't have to use the C library to talk to the kernel; they can call the kernel interface directly—that's what the C library itself does. This ties your code directly to the Linux kernel, making it less portable—but this may not matter to you in an embedded environment. You actually don't have to have any application-layer code at all. It's possible to run your application in the kernel itself as a kernel thread.

For the remainder of this chapter, we'll assume that you're going to use the standard three-layer approach: application, C library, kernel. It's easily the most flexible and portable approach.

Stripping Distributions Versus Building Your Own

The simplest way to build an embedded Linux application is to start with a copy of your favorite commercial Linux distribution that works with your chosen CPU—for example, Red Hat, SuSE, or Debian. Install it onto a hard drive, get it set up so your application starts as part of the initialization process, and call it "done." This can be accomplished in less than a day. If your hardware has the memory and storage space available, this isn't a bad way to go. You lose a lot of control over exactly what goes on in the box, and the result is possibly less robust and secure than a "from scratch" approach, but this might be a tradeoff that you're willing to make for the time saved. This approach can take just a few hours to implement, whereas the other approaches discussed in this book can take days or weeks.

If you're short on storage—but not too short—the next-easiest way to build an embedded application is much like the first: Install a commercial Linux distribution in its most minimal form, and then start ripping out pieces until it fits in the space you have available. Depending on your application's needs, this will work if you have more than about 50MB of storage available. This can probably be done in a day or two, depending on how well you know your chosen distribution.

The third approach is to start with one of the many embedded Linux distributions available on the Internet. It seems as if every day another distribution becomes available for starting embedded projects. Because choosing one can be difficult, I've compiled a list of questions you should think about when looking at the choices. That list is available in Chapter 6, "Embedded Linux Toolkits."

The fourth option is to "roll your own." In days past, this was the solution for most people. With it, you have the greatest control over what your application actually does—but it also takes the most time. You must take great care in choosing the programs you're going to use, and in building your binaries properly so that they'll be as small as possible. However, this is probably the best way to get the smallest possible Linux system in which your application will run.

Static Versus Dynamic Application

The smallest possible embedded Linux application that uses all three software layers (kernel, C library, and application) consists of a kernel loader, the kernel, and a very few statically linked application programs. We'll call this a *static application* because to build it you must link your executables statically against the C library. The great thing about this kind of embedded application is that it's extremely small and very easy to put together if you have only a few executables. In fact, Chapter 8, "Static Application Example: Minicom," shows you how to build a single floppy-disk terminal emulator out of Minicom in about a half hour, by downloading the pieces from the Internet and assembling them. The resulting application is less than 500KB in size and will work on any PC with a serial port.

When the kernel starts up, it runs a program called /linuxrc or /bin/init, depending on whether you use the initrd feature of Linux. If you name your starting executable properly on the root filesystem, you can force the kernel to run it when the kernel's done booting. If you link the executable statically, you don't need to have the shared C libraries in your root filesystem.

Usually, however, you need many executables for your application. Perhaps you need to start the network with ifconfig and route. Perhaps you need certain daemons to run to respond to events. Perhaps you need cron running to provide timing. Each of these programs takes much more space when statically linked than when dynamically linked. So it's best to link executables dynamically if your application has more than a few.

Dynamically linked executables share a single copy of functions that are commonly used in all executables. Examples of functions in the standard C library include printf(), open(), read(), write(), and close(). Sharing the code that performs these common functions helps the embedded programmer in two ways:

- With numerous executables, the total amount of storage used by all the executables plus the shared libraries will be less than the total amount of storage used by the executables if they were statically linked.

- In general, dynamically linked executables take up less real memory for the same reason. There will be only one copy of shared functions, such as printf(), for the whole machine. If the executables are statically linked, each will have its own copy of printf(), and they may both be in memory at the same time even though they're identical.

Dynamically linked executables are marginally slower, however. Because each shared function is not part of the executable code, whenever it's called some fix-up code must discover what actual code needs to be called. This may be only a few dozen instructions, but in a tight loop these instructions can add overhead. Normally, however, the difference is negligible and the storage size win is tremendous.

Software Subsystems

This section examines each of the major software subsystems to determine the best approach to take to optimize them for size.

Kernel Loader

The kernel loader's job is to move the kernel image from long-term storage to memory. Once this job is complete, the loader is no longer needed, and memory that it occupies can be used for other purposes. Because the loader is hardware-specific, there's not much to say about it here, except that in some cases it has to deal with a lot of different device types. If you're really pressed for space, you may be able to remove some code that deals with devices you're not using. Any code removed from the loader is a double win because this code is uncompressed. However, because usually very little code can be cut out, this should be one of the last places you look for code to remove.

initrd

The one feature of the Linux kernel that's most helpful for creating small boot images is the initrd filesystem. Originally intended to simplify the Linux installation process, the initrd filesystem allows a small filesystem to be loaded by the same mechanism that loads the kernel itself from the storage media on which the kernel resides. Best of all, the filesystem is stored in a gzipped format and the kernel uncompresses it to a RAM disk at runtime. This helps the installation process of a standard distribution by eliminating the need for a user to choose a kernel from a list of kernels, each with a different mix of drivers. Before the initrd filesystem was available, there was no way to boot Linux from a device unless the driver was compiled into the kernel. This was especially difficult for x86 PCs using SCSI controllers. Unlike IDE, each type of SCSI controller has its own kernel driver, so the user had to select from among dozens of different kernels before installing Linux. With initrd, a small compressed filesystem— complete with the essential drivers and a boot script—is loaded from the boot media along with the kernel. The kernel uncompresses this filesystem and executes a file within it called /linuxrc. Normally, the script loads the driver required to complete the boot process and exits.

Once the script exits, the initrd filesystem is usually unmounted, its memory is released, and the boot process continues to the real init. However, for an embedded device, there's no reason to exit the initrd filesystem. All the software your embedded application requires can sit in the initrd filesystem, and as long as the /linuxrc executable never exits, the rest of the kernel boot procedure will never happen. This technique offers several significant advantages and two big disadvantages.

These are the advantages:

- If you can get your boot loader to load the kernel, then you can get it to load the initrd filesystem too. They're stored side by side on the media from which the boot loader reads. You can even combine the initrd into the kernel image file, leaving the bootloader with only one file to load.

- Like the kernel, the initrd image is compressed. This drastically reduces the space required to store it on your boot media.

- It's really a RAM disk, so any runtime configuration changes won't survive a power cycle.

And these are the big disadvantages:

- Configuration changes to the initrd filesystem also won't survive a power cycle. This means that any log data or configuration information must be stored separately. You can't just add a new line to /etc/passwd to add a user; any /etc/passwd on your system will be lost during the next power cycle.

- Because it is really a RAM disk, more RAM is required to utilize an initrd. When the initrd is loaded, its entire contents are loaded into memory. When an executable from the initrd is run, a second copy of the executable is loaded into memory to be executed. This means that using an initrd requires more RAM.

Shell

From a command-line point of view, the thing that makes UNIX feel like UNIX is the shell and the utilities. There are two major groupings of UNIX shells: those based on the Bourne shell and those that descend from the C shell. For old timers, discussions of the relative strengths and weaknesses of these shell families can spark religious wars of epic proportions, so we won't go into any detail about which is better. Suffice it to say that for most embedded applications, ash, which is a Bourne shell descendant, is a good shell to start with. Weighing in at about 80KB, it's less than one third of the size of the Linux-standard bash shell. Though it doesn't have nearly the breadth of features of bash, it does have what most programmers need to get the job of a shell done.

You may be wondering what in the world you need a shell for. The shell becomes important if you want to script any of your applications. For example, in the Embedded Linux Workshop in Chapter 7, most of the Web-based administration software is actually written in shell script.

The bottom line is this: If your application is complex, it probably has multiple executables; you'll almost always want to script them in some way, and a shell is the perfect way to do that. The added advantage is that each "executable" you can build with a shell script will probably take only a couple of hundred bytes, but even the smallest dynamically linked C program will take a minimum of a couple of thousand bytes.

C Library

One of the biggest software components of an embedded Linux application is the dynamic libraries. Unless you're linking your executables statically, you'll need the glibc library, at a minimum. Chances are that you'll need other libraries as well.

The glibc library contains the code necessary to most of the standard UNIX functions, such as open(), close(), read(), write(), printf(), and so on. At the time of this writing, once the glibc library is stripped, it's just over 1MB in size. That's really very large for an embedded application, especially since a lot of the code in the library is unnecessary.

Currently there are two ways to reduce the sizes of the libraries required. The most obvious is simply to use another library. As of this writing, there are several contenders to replace the glibc: dietlibc, Newlib, and uClibc. The other technique for reducing the size of the libraries is to remove functions from them that the embedded application won't use. This can be done because all the required executables are known at device build time. Each executable is scanned and a list of used functions is compiled. After all the executables are scanned, any remaining functions that aren't on the list of used functions can be removed with the `objdump` command. Marcus Brinkmann has written a script for the Debian boot floppies called `mklibs.sh` that does just that. Lineo has a similar tool written in Perl called `lipo`, which ships as part of Lineo's SDK.

Utilities

If you're going to write scripts using the shell, as I suggest, then you must have several shell utilities, such as `grep`, `awk`, and `expr`, so that you can write effective scripts.

A great resource for these utilities is BusyBox. Originally written for the Debian install disks, BusyBox has many of the little utilities you need in one small executable. The binary is symbolically linked to each of the programs it can run, so you don't have to do anything strange to your script to use BusyBox. For instance, if you run `grep`, the filesystem looks at the directory entry for `grep`, sees it's a symlink for BusyBox, and loads BusyBox. The BusyBox executable looks at `argv[0]`, sees that it should run the `grep` command, and then runs the BusyBox `grep` command. The reason this works so well is that all the startup and teardown code for an executable is removed—this runs at about 11KB for a stripped executable, which is a substantial savings if you're talking about dozens of programs.

C Compiler

The GNU C compiler has several switches that enable you to choose how it optimizes the object code it produces. *Optimization* in this context refers to both the process of reducing the count of processor instructions, and ordering them correctly so that a given piece of executable code will run as quickly as possible. It's not possible to optimize for both minimum size and maximum speed at the same time.

Compiler Options

When you generate executables for powerful general-purpose computers with lots of memory and disk space, it's usually best to maximize execution speed at the expense of code size. Sometimes it's nice to have debugging information, too. However, when you're building an executable for an embedded application with little memory and little long-term storage, you want to trade execution speed for code size for most of the executables. You may want to make some important executables as fast as possible, but smaller is almost always better.

To show the effects of the various important compiler options, I've compiled the "dhrystone" benchmark in various ways and charted the results of both the size of the compiled output and the speed at which the code ran.

Compiler Option	Short Description	Executable Size	Unlinked Size(.o)	Proc2 Size	Kilo Dhrystones/ Sec
	No options used	15514	4888	80	369
-O2	Optimize for speed a lot	14522	3896	56	531
-O3	Optimize for speed a whole lot	14554	3952	56	544
-Os	Optimize for size	14424	3840	48	643
-m386	Only use 80386 instructions (not 486 or Pentium)	15514	4888	80	369
-mpentium	Only use Pentium instructions	15514	4888	80	368
-g	Include debug info	36390	27960	80	369
-static	Link everything in the executable binary	967612	4888	80	360

Each of the options has a different effect on the size of the compiled output. Most of these options work to some degree on all chipsets, with the obvious exception of the -m386 and -mpentium switches.

-Ox Options

The GNU C Compiler comes with lots of online documentation, but it can be somewhat difficult to find, and even more difficult to navigate once you find it. The info gcc command starts the GNU info command, displaying the documentation for the GNU C Compiler. The GNU C Compiler command has these optimization options:

- **-O0**

  Don't optimize.

- **-O1**

  Optimize. Optimizing compilation takes somewhat more time, and a lot more memory for a large function.

  Without -O, the compiler's goal is to reduce the cost of compilation and to make debugging produce the expected results. Statements are independent; if you stop the program with a breakpoint between statements, you can then assign a new value to any variable or change the program counter to any other statement in the function and get exactly the results you would expect from the source code.

Without -O, the compiler only allocates variables declared `register` in registers. The resulting compiled code is a little worse than produced by the GNU C Compiler without -O.

With -O, the compiler tries to reduce code size and execution time.

When you specify -O, the compiler turns on -fthread-jumps and -fdefer-pop on all machines. The compiler turns on -fdelayed-branch on machines that have delay slots, and -fomit-frame-pointer on machines that can support debugging even without a frame pointer. On some machines, the compiler also turns on other flags.

- **-02**

  Optimize even more. The GNU C Compiler performs nearly all supported optimizations that don't involve a space/speed tradeoff. The compiler doesn't perform loop unrolling or function inlining when you specify -02. As compared to -O, this option increases both compilation time and the performance of the generated code.

  -02 turns on all optional optimizations except for loop unrolling and function inlining. It also turns on the -fforce-mem option on all machines and frame-pointer elimination on machines where doing so doesn't interfere with debugging.

- **-03**

  Optimize yet more. -03 turns on all optimizations specified by -02 and also turns on the `inline-functions` option.

- **-Os**

  Optimize for size. -Os enables all -02 optimizations that don't typically increase code size. It also performs further optimizations designed to reduce code size. Most of the time, the -Os choice is best for embedded applications. Unfortunately, this means that you have to compile most of your binaries yourself. It also means you have to change most `configure` scripts or their generated Makefiles. It would be helpful if application writers would make it standard practice to add a --configure-small option to `configure`.

No Optimization Versus -O3 or -Os

`Proc2()` is one of the important functions in the dhrystone benchmark (see Listings 2.1 through 2.4). It's called by one of the inner loops and itself has a loop that can run numerous times. Even if you don't have an assembly language background, you can get an idea of the complexity of the i386 assembly code instructions produced by compiling this loop at the different optimization levels to see how the C compiler reduces the number of instructions necessary to arrive at the same result.

Listing 2.1   **C Code**

```c
int IntGlob;
char Char1Glob;

void Proc2(int *IntParIO){
  int IntLoc;
  int EnumLoc;

  IntLoc = *IntParIO + 10;
  for (;;) {
    if (Char1Glob == 'A') {
      --IntLoc;
      *IntParIO = IntLoc - IntGlob;
      EnumLoc = 1;
    }
    if (EnumLoc == 1) break;
  }
}
```

Listing 2.2   **No Optimization (80 Bytes)**

```
000005a8 <Proc2>:
  5a8: push    %ebp
  5a9: mov     %esp,%ebp
  5ab: sub     $0x8,%esp
  5ae: push    %ebx
  5af: mov     0x8(%ebp),%eax
  5b2: mov     (%eax),%ebx
  5b4: add     $0xa,%ebx
  5b7: mov     %ebx,0xfffffffc(%ebp)
  5ba: lea     0x0(%esi),%esi
  5c0: cmpb    $0x41,0x0
  5c7: jne     5e5 <Proc2+0x3d>
  5c9: decl    0xfffffffc(%ebp)
  5cc: mov     0x8(%ebp),%eax
  5cf: mov     0xfffffffc(%ebp),%edx
  5d2: mov     0x0,%ecx
  5d8: mov     %edx,%ebx
  5da: sub     %ecx,%ebx
  5dc: mov     %ebx,(%eax)
  5de: movl    $0x1,0xfffffff8(%ebp)
  5e5: cmpl    $0x1,0xfffffff8(%ebp)
  5e9: jne     5f0 <Proc2+0x48>
  5eb: jmp     5f2 <Proc2+0x4a>
  5ed: lea     0x0(%esi),%esi
  5f0: jmp     5c0 <Proc2+0x18>
  5f2: mov     0xfffffff4(%ebp),%ebx
  5f5: leave
  5f6: ret
  5f7: nop
```

Listing 2.3   *-O3* (56 Bytes)

```
000003d4 <Proc2>:
 3d4: push    %ebp
 3d5: mov     %esp,%ebp
 3d7: push    %esi
 3d8: push    %ebx
 3d9: mov     0x8(%ebp),%ebx
 3dc: mov     (%ebx),%edx
 3de: add     $0xa,%edx
 3e1: mov     0x0,%al
 3e6: cmp     $0x41,%al
 3e8: jne     3fa <Proc2+0x26>
 3ea: dec     %edx
 3eb: mov     %edx,%esi
 3ed: sub     0x0,%esi
 3f3: mov     %esi,(%ebx)
 3f5: mov     $0x1,%ecx
 3fa: mov     0x0,%al
 3ff: cmp     $0x1,%ecx
 402: jne     3e6 <Proc2+0x12>
 404: lea     0xfffffff8(%ebp),%esp
 407: pop     %ebx
 408: pop     %esi
 409: leave
 40a: ret
 40b: nop
```

Listing 2.4   *-Os* (48 Bytes)

```
00000374 <Proc2>:
 374: push    %ebp
 375: mov     %esp,%ebp
 377: push    %ebx
 378: mov     0x8(%ebp),%ecx
 37b: mov     (%ecx),%eax
 37d: add     $0xa,%eax
 380: cmpb    $0x41,0x0
 387: jne     399 <Proc2+0x25>
 389: dec     %eax
 38a: mov     %eax,%ebx
 38c: sub     0x0,%ebx
 392: mov     %ebx,(%ecx)
 394: mov     $0x1,%edx
 399: cmp     $0x1,%edx
 39c: jne     380 <Proc2+0xc>
 39e: mov     0xfffffffc(%ebp),%ebx
 3a1: leave
 3a2: ret
 3a3: nop
```

–i386

The -i386 option causes the compiler to assume that the object code is going to run on an Intel 80386 (as opposed to an 80486, Pentium, AMD, and so on). This affects instruction choice, ordering, and alignment. Normally, you'll want to choose the 80386 execution model even if you're running your application on a higher-level processor. You won't get the optimal performance out of your processor, but you'll get the smallest code footprint. If you have a small number of executables that comprise the bulk of the processing for your application, you may want to compile those particular executables with the option for the chipset you're really running.

If you're running on a non-x86 processor, don't use this option. Instead, look at the processor-specific documentation in the compiler documentation (info gcc), and choose the smallest execution model for your processor.

–g

Many packages automatically compile with the -g switch set. This option tells the compiler to include debug symbols so that you can trace through the code at the source level with the GNU debugger. The executable that the compiler produces is about twice the size of an executable created without this switch.

Once your program is working, you probably won't have a chance to debug it while it's in your embedded appliance, so it's best to get rid of all debug symbols before you ship the code. There are a few ways to do that. You can strip the code of the debug symbols when moving it from its default compiled location with the strip command, remove the -g option from the Makefile, or compile with the -s option to inform ld to omit all symbol information from the output file. Unfortunately, this still leaves in place the .note and .comment ELF sections, and so you will still want to do a 'strip -remove-section=.note --remove-section=.comment file'.

–static

If any of your executables are compiled with the -static switch, they'll be gigantic compared to those without the -static switch. For comparison, the dhrystone executable compiled with the -Os switch was 14424 bytes long. The executable compiled with the -static switch was 967612 bytes long—more than 67 times larger! The only time you might want to include a static executable in an embedded application is when you want that to be the only executable that runs. For details on this special case, see Chapter 8.

Surprising Results

The results of the dhrystone benchmark are quite surprising. First of all, there was no difference in size or speed of the executables compiled with the -m386, -mpentium, and no optimization switches at all. In fact, the executables produced using these options were identical.

However, the most surprising result was that the code optimized for size ran so much faster than even those supposedly optimized for speed. The highest speed optimization level (-O3) resulted in 544 kilo-dhrystones per second on my 500 MHz Pentium III compiled with gcc version egcs-2.91.66 19990314/Linux (egcs-1.1.2 release). That's pretty good—47% faster than with no optimization at all. However, the -Os option, which is supposed to produce code that's smaller but not necessarily faster than -O3, produced code that's 18% faster than the -O3 code, which comes to a whopping 74% faster than with no optimization at all!

Summary

There are a few important concepts to glean from this chapter:

- Size does matter when you're working on embedded applications.
- To build the smallest, most reliable embedded application, you must either choose an embedded Linux distribution that matches your needs or roll your own.
- In all but the simplest applications, you should use the dynamic C libraries (shared libraries) as opposed to statically linking your executables.
- Don't use -g or -static when compiling your executables for inclusion in an embedded application. Use -static only when there will be a single executable in your embedded system. Always use -Os optimization.

3

Software Configuration

CONFIGURING A NEWLY INSTALLED LINUX COMPUTER based on a standard distribution is a time-consuming task. Yet, if you're going to use that computer on the Internet, it's crucial that you configure it correctly. If you leave lots of default services running with weak or nonexistent security, it's just a matter of time before some cracker gets into your box and defaces it—or worse, destroys it.

The author speaks from experience.

Be Selective About Software

One day, during the summer of 2000, with my son in the hospital and a project at work falling apart, I got an email from my Internet service provider saying, in effect, "Don't look now, but your server has been cracked." Sure enough, some cracker had replaced the home page on my two-week-old Red Hat 6.2 system with a long diatribe extolling the virtues of the Esperanto language, complete with pointers to www.esperanto.org so I could find out more. Since I was running between work and hospital and home, I really didn't have time to fix things properly, so I just changed all the passwords on the system and removed the cracker's new home page.

That just made him mad.

A week later, I found that the Web server would no longer work at all. The cracker got in again, built numerous backdoors into the system, and tweaked things so that the

Web server wouldn't start. He changed the definition of /dev/null so that when Apache read from it, it would block. This took a while to find, and would have been almost impossible without the strace command. (By the way, if you're a developer and you've never used strace, you're missing out on a powerful debugging tool.)

This time I got serious about battening down the machine. I completely reinstalled Linux and upgraded all the software to the newest, most secure versions. Almost as important, I reviewed each service the computer was running, and disabled the ones I didn't need. When I was done, the machine had almost no open TCP or UDP ports.

The moral of this story is that it's crucial to choose wisely the software that will run on your embedded system. Ship only the software that you need to run, and be sure to configure it properly. Don't simply use the default configuration files that ship with server software; they're often set up so that it's easy to get the software up and running by ignoring the security issues.

Tip: One of the best resources for securing a Linux server system is David Ranch's TrinityOS. See www.ecst.csuchico.edu/~dranch/LINUX/index-linux.html#trinityos for details.

Dealing with Software Expectations

In an embedded environment, making wise choices about the software that runs on your device comes somewhat naturally—you're very concerned about how much space your software takes up, so you probably don't have a lot of extra servers clogging up the boot flash anyway.

But configuration is a different story. In general, configuring a Linux system is difficult. Each service usually wants its own configuration file. Each configuration file has a different syntax. Many configuration files want to live somewhere in the /etc tree, but others don't. For all of these reasons, replicating a Linux system is especially difficult—where do you get all of the files?

Configuring an embedded system addresses all these issues and adds a few of its own. Each program that runs on the embedded device expects to find its configuration file in a certain location in the directory tree. Some locations may not be writeable because they live in a read-only filesystem. Others may be in a RAM filesystem, so any changes will be lost during the next reboot. Writing several configuration files to flash memory implies that a filesystem must be on that flash, which adds complexity.

Symlinking Configuration Files

The solution to configuration files being spread across many directory trees is fairly easy; for each configuration file, create a symbolic link pointing to a file in a single directory that houses all the configuration files. A good name for this directory is /config.

For example, let's say that your application needs to be able to change the values stored in the `resolv.conf` and `syslog.conf` files as part of its normal operations. Both of these files normally reside in the `/etc` directory. However, the `/etc` directory also contains many files that you'll never need to change but do need to exist, such as the `hosts` and `services` files. Instead of storing the contents of `resolv.conf` and `syslog.conf` in the `/etc` directory, you can simply create symlinks called `/etc/resolv.conf` and `/etc/syslog.conf` that point to `/config/resolv.conf` and `/config/syslog.conf`, respectively.

This concept is quite powerful. The `/config` directory can then be mounted on a different device from the rest of the root filesystem. This way, the root can consist of a smaller read-only filesystem, and the `/config` filesystem can live in flash and be read/write. Each configuration file *looks* like it lives where the server software expects it to live, but in reality it can be changed at will by the configuration software.

The Embedded Linux Workshop takes this concept one step further. Instead of having multiple configuration files in one read/write directory, there is a single configuration file that can either live in a single read/write directory or, using a simple kernel driver, in raw flash memory. There are several advantages to centralizing the configuration information to a single file:

- You don't have to have a full flash filesystem to store a single file.

- Your configuration software doesn't have to understand how to modify all the different types of configuration files in existence. Most configuration files are meant for humans to modify, not computer programs, so they're difficult to change programmatically.

- A single configuration file makes replicating an embedded device simple—copy a single file from one machine to the other.

- A simple *name=value* structure works for most situations. This structure is easily understandable by humans and easily parsable and modifiable by computers.

Resolving Software Expectation Conflicts

There's still one problem with this approach; the software programs that require the configuration files expect them to be in a certain form. The `syslogd` program, for example, won't know what to do with the *name=value* syntax used by the Embedded Linux Workshop's single configuration file.

There are basically two approaches to resolving this problem:

- Modify the programs so that they can use the single configuration file directly.

- Using the information in the single Embedded Linux Workshop configuration file, create the configuration file(s) that the program expects to see.

For the most part, I use the second approach for the Embedded Linux Workshop. I believe that the fewer changes made to the individual components of an embedded project (syslogd, for example), the better. Here's why:

- If it was working when you got it, and you didn't touch it, it should still work in the field.

- Changing software such as syslogd is difficult and error-prone if you're not already familiar with the software. However, creating the syslogd.conf file out of *name=value* pairs from the single configuration file is relatively easy.

- If you change the syslogd software to read its configuration information directly from the single configuration file, that's a substantial change that you'll have to keep track of forever. If you need to upgrade to a later version of syslogd in the future, you'll have to create and apply a patch to the new version, fixing any problems in software you may not have seen for a while. On the other hand, if you use the second approach—creating the configuration file(s) that the software expects to see—and the configuration file syntax has not changed in the new version, you have no work to do when you upgrade versions.

There are a few drawbacks to building the configuration file(s) that the software expects to see rather than changing the software to use the single configuration file. First, your boot time will be slower than it could be. Probably not by much, but still—slower. Second, the custom configuration file(s) will take up more room on your embedded device. The software to create the application-specific configuration file and the configuration file itself both take up room that may be extremely valuable, depending on the size of your embedded device. You can normally remove the application-specific configuration file once the software that needs it is finished reading it, but doing so adds complexity to your startup code.

There is ample precedent for using a single configuration file for the entire computer. The most well-known example of this approach is the Registry in Microsoft Windows. Even with all its shortcomings, the Windows Registry has made life easier for developers and users alike by moving all configuration information to a central, searchable location. To get an idea of how the single-configuration file concept works in practice, let's take a look at two examples from the Embedded Linux Workshop: the network setup code and the resolver setup code.

When the machine in this example boots, it stays in initrd mode, so the first user space code to run is a script named linuxrc. The job of this script is to set up the runtime environment. Part of that setup code calls each of the startup scripts for the various packages, much like the /etc/rc.d/rc3.d scripts in a Red Hat system. Listing 3.1 shows the code within linuxrc that runs the startup scripts.

Listing 3.1   **Part of the */linuxrc* Script**

```
. /mnt/envi
for x in `(cd /etc/rc;echo S*)`;do
    echo Starting $x...
    /etc/rc/$x
done
```

The first line of the script loads the configuration file. The configuration file is set up so that any shell script that needs its contents can simply source it in with the dot (.) command, and all the *name=value* pairs are loaded into shell variables. The rest of the linuxrc script finds the names of each of the files in the /etc/rc directory that begin with *S*, and runs them. The two scripts that we're going to look at are S14resolv (see Listing 3.2) and S15network.

Listing 3.2   **The *S14resolv* Script**

```
 1   #!/bin/sh
 2   ######################################################################
 3   # Set up the DNS resolver
 4   ######################################################################
 5   [ -z "$RESOLV_CONF" ] && RESOLV_CONF=/etc/resolv.conf
 6
 7   rm -f $RESOLV_CONF
 8   [ -n "$RESOLV_IP0" ] && echo "nameserver $RESOLV_IP0" >> $RESOLV_CONF
 9   [ -n "$RESOLV_IP1" ] && echo "nameserver $RESOLV_IP1" >> $RESOLV_CONF
10   [ -n "$RESOLV_IP2" ] && echo "nameserver $RESOLV_IP2" >> $RESOLV_CONF
11   [ -n "$RESOLV_IP3" ] && echo "nameserver $RESOLV_IP3" >> $RESOLV_CONF
```

The S14resolv script's job is to set up the Linux system so that applications running within the embedded box are able to resolve network names using DNS. It does so by first deleting (line 7), and then building up (lines 8–10) the /etc/resolv.conf file from values in the single configuration file. To make all of this work, the configuration file has a line that looks like this:

```
export RESOLV_IP0="4.2.2.1"
```

After the S14resolv script completes, the /etc/resolv.conf file has a single line:

```
nameserver 4.2.2.1
```

If we had named RESOLV_IP1, RESOLV_IP2, or RESOLV_IP3 within the configuration file, the /etc/resolv.conf file would have had more nameserver lines to reflect the multiple DNS name servers we can access.

Next, we'll look at a much more complex example, S15network (see Listing 3.3). The S15network script does most of the work when bringing up the network:

- Sets up the localhost.

- Can support up to 10 network connections.

- Allows for routing and masquerading between networks.
- Begins the setup of ipchains for firewall rules.
- Optionally sets up a default route.
- Uses the newer ip command instead of ifconfig/route to conserve space.

Listing 3.3 **The *S15network* Script**

```
1  #!/bin/sh
2  ###################################################################
3  # Start IP networking
4  ###################################################################
5
6  ###################################################################
7  # conf: Configure a network interface
8  # $1    NETIF      (eth0)
9  # $2    NETIP      (192.168.0.1)
10 # $3    NETNAM     (WAN/LAN/dmz/etc)
11 # $4    NETMASK    (255.255.255.0)
12 # $4    NETOPT     (MTU=1500 promisc)
13 # $5    NETDEF     (""=no !""=ip address of gateway)
14 ###################################################################
15 conf () {
16   NETEN=$1; shift
17   NETIF=$1; shift
18   NETIP=$1; shift
19   NETNAM=$1; shift
20   NETMASK=$1; shift
21   NETOPT=$1; shift
22   NETDEF=$1; shift
23   NETMASQ=$1; shift
24   if [ -n "$NETIP" ] && [ "$NETEN" = "1" ]; then
25     NETMASK=`ipcalc -m $NETIP $NETMASK`        # Calc deflt if no mask
26     NETBITS=`ipcalc -t $NETIP $NETMASK`
27     BROADCAST=`ipcalc -b $NETIP $NETMASK`
28     NETWORK=`ipcalc -n $NETIP $NETMASK`
29
30     # bring up the nic
31     ip address add $NETIP/$NETBITS broadcast $BROADCAST dev $NETIF
32     if [ "$?" != "0" ]; then
33       echo "$NETNAM ($NETIP-$NETIF): failed (ip address add)"
34       return 1
35     fi
36     ip link set dev $NETIF up
37     if [ "$?" != "0" ]; then
38       echo "$NETNAM ($NETIP-$NETIF): failed (ip link up)"
39       return 1
40     fi
41     [ "$NETOPT" != "" ] && $NETOPT
42
```

```
43        # give it the default route
44        if [ -n "$NETDEF" ]; then
45          ip route add default via $NETDEF
46          if [ "$?" != "0" ]; then
47            echo "$NETNAM ($NETIP-$NETIF): failed (default route)"
48            return 1
49          fi
50        fi
51
52        # Masquerade this network?
53        if [ "$NETMASQ" = "1" ]; then
54          ipchcnf del $NETNAM-masq
55          ipchcnf add $NETNAM-masq -A forward -s $NETWORK/$NETMASK -j MASQ
56        fi
57
58        # And we're up!
59        echo "$NETNAM ($NETIP-$NETIF): up"
60      fi
61    return 0
62  }
63
64  # Retry client's connect attempts
65  # See: /usr/src/linux/Documentation/networking/ip_dynaddr.txt
66  # ----------------------------------------------------------
67  echo "1" > /proc/sys/net/ipv4/ip_dynaddr
68
69  # Enable routing, but force specific forward rules
70  # ------------------------------------------------
71  ipchains --policy forward REJECT
72  echo "1" > /proc/sys/net/ipv4/ip_forward
73
74  # Configure global masquerading
75  # -----------------------------
76  ipchains -S 7200 10 60
77
78  # Configure localhost
79  # -------------------
80  #ifconfig lo 127.0.0.1 netmask 255.0.0.0 broadcast 127.255.255.255
81  #route add -net 127.0.0.0 netmask 255.0.0.0 lo
82  ip address add 127.0.0.1/8 broadcast 127.255.255.255 dev lo
83  ip link set dev lo up
84
85  # Configure network
86  # -----------------
87  conf   "$NETEN0" "$NETIF0" "$NETIP0" "$NETNAM0" \
88         "$NETMASK0" "$NETOPT0" "$NETDEF0" "$NETMASQ0"
89  conf   "$NETEN1" "$NETIF1" "$NETIP1" "$NETNAM1" \
90         "$NETMASK1" "$NETOPT1" "$NETDEF1" "$NETMASQ1"
91  conf   "$NETEN2" "$NETIF2" "$NETIP2" "$NETNAM2" \
92         "$NETMASK2" "$NETOPT2" "$NETDEF2" "$NETMASQ2"
93  conf   "$NETEN3" "$NETIF3" "$NETIP3" "$NETNAM3" \
```

continues

Listing 3.3   **Continued**

```
94          "$NETMASK3" "$NETOPT3" "$NETDEF3" "$NETMASQ3"
95  conf    "$NETEN4" "$NETIF4" "$NETIP4" "$NETNAM4" \
96          "$NETMASK4" "$NETOPT4" "$NETDEF4" "$NETMASQ4"
97  conf    "$NETEN5" "$NETIF5" "$NETIP5" "$NETNAM5" \
98          "$NETMASK5" "$NETOPT5" "$NETDEF5" "$NETMASQ5"
99  conf    "$NETEN6" "$NETIF6" "$NETIP6" "$NETNAM6" \
100         "$NETMASK6" "$NETOPT6" "$NETDEF1" "$NETMASQ6"
101 conf    "$NETEN7" "$NETIF7" "$NETIP7" "$NETNAM7" \
102         "$NETMASK7" "$NETOPT7" "$NETDEF7" "$NETMASQ7"
103 conf    "$NETEN8" "$NETIF8" "$NETIP8" "$NETNAM8" \
104         "$NETMASK8" "$NETOPT8" "$NETDEF8" "$NETMASQ8"
105 conf    "$NETEN9" "$NETIF9" "$NETIP9" "$NETNAM9" \
106         "$NETMASK9" "$NETOPT9" "$NETDEF9" "$NETMASQ9"
```

The S15network script has three major parts:

- Lines 15–62 comprise the conf() function.
- Lines 64–83 set up various files in the /proc filesystem and initialize the firewall and localhost.
- Lines 87–106 call the conf() function to set up each of the network interfaces.

Let's trace the following sample configuration through the S15network script:

```
export NETEN0=1
export NETNAM0="wan"
export NETIF0="eth0"
export NETIP0="192.168.0.9"
export NETDEF0="192.168.0.1"

export NETEN1=1
export NETNAM1="lan"
export NETIF1="eth1"
export NETIP1="192.168.10.9"
```

Lines 15–62 define the conf() function and are of no consequence until later in the script.

Lines 67 and 72 set different kernel flags by writing to special files in the /proc filesystem. Line 67 tells the kernel to retry the connection that caused a network session to activate—usually a PPP connection. Line 72 tells the kernel that it can forward packets between network connections. However, line 71 sets up the default firewall rule to *not* allow forwards between network connections. If any forwards are required, they must be set up later with specific firewall rules.

Line 76 sets up good defaults for masquerade timeouts.

Lines 82–83 set up the loopback interface.

Finally, we get to the configuration of the network interfaces. In our example, we have two network interfaces, eth0 (named wan) and eth1 (named lan). Because we only have two, only the first two calls to the conf() function (lines 87–88 and 89–90) are of any consequence.

The first call to `conf()` on lines 87–88 sets up the `eth0` (wan) interface. Lines 16–23 extract the local variables from the function call. Line 24 tests to make sure that the interface is enabled and that an IP address is assigned. Lines 25–28 use an external C program, `ipcalc`, to calculate the network address, network mask, and network bits.

Lines 31–35 assign the IP address and network information for the interface, and then deal with any error(s) returned. Similarly, lines 36–40 actually bring up the link and check for errors.

Line 41 is a bit of a kludge. A previous evolution of this script used `ifconfig/route` instead of the `ip` command. The `NETOPT` variable was used to give `ifconfig` any extra parameters (such as an MTU setting). Since the syntax of the `ip` command is different from that of the `ifconfig` command, the same technique won't work for both. I decided to just redefine the `NETOPT` as a separate command. With it, you can do whatever you need (such as set the MTU of an interface).

Lines 44–50 set up the default route, and lines 53–56 set up IP masquerading.

After studying the code, you may be a bit worried about security. For instance, the `NETOPT` variable simply runs a command—any command. Similarly, the `NETDEF` variable could be set to `"some.ip.address; rm -rf /"`, which would blow away the machine on line 45. For the Embedded Linux Workshop, I've taken the stance that the data in the configuration file is trustworthy. Verification is done in the software that builds and/or modifies the configuration file, since this software must be secure anyway.

The second call to `conf()` sets up the `eth1` (lan) interface. The specifics for the `conf()` function are very similar to those for the `eth0` (wan) interface, except that the default interface is already set up, so the test on line 44 is not activated.

Summary

Setting up a Linux system is quite complex. Much of that complexity stems from the fact that there are so many configuration files spread across the directory tree, each of which has a unique syntax. Programmers who want to create an embedded application can make their job a lot easier by planning out how to configure the machine, both at build time and runtime.

4

Booting Your Embedded Linux Device

Conceptually, booting an embedded device is very simple:

1. Initialize the hardware.
2. Ready the root filesystem.
3. Load the kernel from the boot media.
4. Jump into the kernel.

The kernel takes it from here; it configures memory, its drivers take possession of the hardware they're interested in, and so on. Once the kernel is satisfied that it has taken care of everything, it starts up the userspace init process, which runs any other processes that are needed.

Like many things in life, however, even though booting the device is conceptually quite simple, the devil is in the details. This chapter looks at those details—answering the question, "How does the Linux kernel move from the boot media to running in RAM?"

Understanding the Boot Process

Typically, a computer boots in three stages:

1. The hardware is initialized by software closely tied to the hardware.

2. The kernel is loaded into RAM by the kernel loader.

3. The kernel itself runs, further initializing the hardware, and then runs the application software.

BIOS

When power is applied to an embedded Linux device, the hardware goes through a series of events that ends with the processor in some sort of reset state. When the hardware releases the processor from the reset state, it begins executing instructions at a known location. These instructions are normally stored in ROM or flash memory. On a PC, these instructions are called the *BIOS*. The BIOS code is responsible for getting the hardware on the PC ready for the operating system. As part of this setup process, the early BIOS code does a number of really low-level things such as enabling L1 and L2 caches, detecting how much memory is installed, and setting up the RAM refresh. If you're writing this code, you'll have your nose deeply buried in the user manuals for your processor, your processor's supporting chipset, and the devices you're setting up. After the initial chipset and hardware initialization, the BIOS then loads the kernel (or the kernel loader) into memory and starts it running. On a PC, once Linux is running it generally ignores the BIOS, so in this book we'll also ignore all the BIOS functionality used by other operating systems such as Microsoft Windows but ignored by Linux. Linux also runs on many architectures, such as ARM, MIPS, PowerPC, and so on, which don't use a PC BIOS. Generally these other architectures have some architecture-specific sort of low-level startup code (such as PPCBug, OpenFirmware, RedBoot, and so on) that provides functionality similar to what's provided by the PC BIOS. For the rest of this book, we'll call this startup code the "BIOS," with the understanding that we're really talking about whatever low-level firmware code is appropriate for the architecture.

Kernel Loader

The kernel loader is a small program that has a better understanding of the rules of the operating system and mass storage layout than the BIOS. It can therefore load the OS and start it. On an x86 PC running a standard Linux desktop distribution such as Red Hat, SuSe, or Debian, a kernel loader such as LILO or GRUB normally loads the kernel. For x86-based embedded applications, `syslinux` also works very well.

For non-x86-based architectures, other boot loaders such as MILO may be needed. If you're writing a BIOS from scratch, or using a system that was specifically designed with Linux in mind, the kernel loader may very well be integrated directly into the BIOS. Regardless of how it happens on your specific platform, after the kernel loader completes its job, the kernel is in memory and the loader jumps into it.

Kernel

Immediately after the kernel loader jumps into the Linux kernel, the kernel starts initializing itself and all of its compiled-in drivers. If a monitor is attached to the computer (or a serial console is enabled), the first thing the kernel says looks something like this:

```
Linux version 2.2.18-20 (root@porky.devel.redhat.com)
(gcc version egcs-2.91.66+19990314/Linux (egcs-1.1.2 release)) #1
Mon Nov 23 10:25:54 EDT 2000
```

This list gives you the Linux version, the user and machine for which the kernel was compiled, the compiler version, and the kernel compile date. (So much detail that we had to break it into three lines above.) A lot of information about the kernel boot process comes next. Each of the compiled-in drivers typically prints out some information about itself. After the kernel is completely initialized, the computer is finally ready to run the embedded application.

In Linux, as in any version of UNIX, the software that runs can be either kernel code or a user process. If the processor has a Memory Management Unit (MMU), user code runs at a lower privilege level than kernel code, which prevents it from doing things that could crash the computer. Linux can also run on computers without an MMU (using the uClinux kernel patches). In these cases, there's no concept of differing privilege levels—all code essentially runs as if it were kernel code and has the potential to crash the machine. While this can make debugging more difficult than usual, it shouldn't deter developers from considering the less expensive MMU-less processors. Since users typically don't put arbitrary software on their embedded device (as they do on their PCs), an embedded device is much less crash-prone. The software was put there by the embedded system designer and presumably was well tested.

An embedded application will usually consist of one or more user-level applications, the first of which is called init. As shown in Listing 4.1, kernel code from the /usr/src/linux/init/main.c file, the program doesn't have to be called init; you can pass an init=/some_program command-line argument into the kernel from the boot loader and the program you specified will run at boot time.

Listing 4.1   **Kernel Code from** */usr/src/linux/init/main.c*

```
static int init(void * unused)
{
    lock_kernel();
    do_basic_setup();

    /*
     * Ok, we have completed the initial bootup, and
     * we're essentially up and running. Get rid of the
     * initmem segments and start the user-mode stuff.
     */
    free_initmem();
    unlock_kernel();
```

continues

Listing 4.1   **Continued**

```
    if (open("/dev/console", O_RDWR, 0) < 0)
        printk("Warning: unable to open an initial console.\n");

    (void) dup(0);
    (void) dup(0);

    /*
     * We try each of these until one succeeds.
     *
     * The Bourne shell can be used instead of init if we are
     * trying to recover a really broken machine.
     */

    if (execute_command)
        execve(execute_command,argv_init,envp_init);
        execve("/sbin/init",argv_init,envp_init);
        execve("/etc/init",argv_init,envp_init);
        execve("/bin/init",argv_init,envp_init);
        execve("/bin/sh",argv_init,envp_init);
    panic("No init found.  Try passing init= option to kernel.");
}
```

In a typical Linux desktop or server computer, the init program reads a file called /etc/inittab. This file enumerates which scripts and commands init needs to run to achieve the required runlevel, effectively booting the machine. However, you don't have to use the standard init program that reads inittab and boots the machine; the init program can do anything you want in your embedded system. In fact, if you statically link it, it can be the only file on the filesystem. Your entire application can be housed in this single program. For a deeply embedded system with little need to talk to the outside world, this may be the way to go. Using this technique, you'll get the smallest possible disk image.

More typically, however, you'll want to use a small shell, such as ash, and run some scripts that use external commands on your filesystem to do things such as bring up the network and run any daemons your application requires. This is the technique used in the Embedded Linux Workshop (see Chapter 7).

Sample BIOS and Boot Loader

The best way to get a good sense of what's really going on when the processor gets control of the machine during power-on is to take a look at some code. Fortunately, several Open Source projects are attempting to produce a usable BIOS for the x86 architecture. Each project is quite young at the time of this writing, so the state of these projects may be different as you read these words. However, even though the filenames and locations referenced here may change, the code itself essentially won't.

The code requirements at this level haven't changed much since the i386 was introduced many years ago.

LinuxBIOS

Let's take a close look at a few files from the LinuxBIOS project. The stated goals of the LinuxBIOS project are as follows (adapted from the LinuxBIOS home page at `http://www.acl.lanl.gov/linuxbios/`):

What is LinuxBIOS?

We are working on making Linux our BIOS. In other words, we plan to replace the BIOS in NVRAM on our motherboards with a Linux image, and instead of running the BIOS on startup we'll run Linux. We have a number of reasons for doing this:

- We want our cluster nodes to come up [and] go out to the net for direction on how they should boot (diskless, local disk, reload, etc.). While there is a standard for this (PXE from Intel), it has a lot of limitations.

- By far the most important function of the BIOS is to support obsolete code, such as DOS. Modern operating systems such as Linux have absolutely no use for what the BIOS does. Still worse, many BIOSes do a poor job of configuring the PCI bus for systems such as Linux. Replacing the BIOS with Linux allows faster reboots and better system configuration.

- The NVRAM can be written with the kernel we most commonly use. We can envision booting Linux in 10 milliseconds or so—a very attractive idea.

How will it work?

1. When the PC exits the RESET state, it starts executing instructions at location 0xffff:0. At this point, the Pentium is emulating a 20-year-old microprocessor, the 16-bit 8086. This address is in NVRAM. We will have rewritten NVRAM with a stub of LinuxBIOS.

2. We initialize the chipset so that interrupts work, and DRAM is on.

3. As soon as we have DRAM we turn on the GDT and jump to 32-bit assembly code.

4. 32-bit assembly code does a bit more work and jumps to C.

5. The C code is short: it uncompresses the Linux image out of NVRAM into RAM and jumps to it.

License

Parts of the code in the rest of this chapter are covered under the GPL; others are covered under the following license:

> This software and ancillary information (herein called SOFTWARE) called LinuxBIOS is made available under the terms described here. The SOFTWARE has been approved for release with associated LA-CC Number 00-34. Unless otherwise indicated, this SOFTWARE has been authored by an employee or employees of the University of California, operator of the Los Alamos National Laboratory under Contract No. W-7405-ENG-36 with the U.S. Department of Energy. The U.S. Government has rights to use, reproduce, and distribute this SOFTWARE. The public may copy, distribute, prepare derivative works and publicly display this SOFTWARE without charge, provided that this Notice and any statement of authorship are reproduced on all copies. Neither the Government nor the University makes any warranty, express or implied, or assumes any liability or responsibility for the use of this SOFTWARE. If SOFTWARE is modified to produce derivative works, such modified SOFTWARE should be clearly marked, so as not to confuse it with the version available from LANL. Copyright 2000, Ron Minnich, Advanced Computing Lab, LANL rminnich@lanl.gov

Startup Code

Several chipsets are supported by the LinuxBIOS project. This chapter shows the startup code for the SIS630—an arbitrary choice. Note that the source code has been cleaned up a bit, removing numerous `#ifdefs` that are not relevant to the discussion. From `linuxbios/SIS630/crt0.S` and `chip/intel/intel_start32.S`:

```
/*
 * This is the entry code--the mkrom(8) utility makes a jumpvector
 * to this address.
 *
 * When we get here we are in x86 real mode.
 *
 *      %cs     = 0xf000        %ip     = 0x0000
 *      %ds     = 0x0000        %es     = 0x0000
 *      %dx     = 0x0yxx        (y = 3 for i386, 5 for pentium, 6 for P6,
 *                                      where x is undefined)
 *      %fl     = 0x0002
 */
```

This first instruction, at location 0xffff:0, jumps around the Global Descriptor Table (GDT) data area:

```
_start: jmp _realstart
```

The next bit of memory has both a pointer to the GDT (gdtptr) and the GDT
itself (gdt). The lgdt (Load Global Descriptor Table Register) instruction, after the
_realstart label below, points to this space. The Global Descriptor Table defines
the translation between physical and virtual memory for the kernel.

```
/* We have modified this from the original freebios to make it
 * compatible with Linux. This puts text at seg 0x10 and data at 0x18
 */
gdtptr:
        .word   4*8-1
        .long   gdt                     /* we know the offset */
gdt:
        .word   0x0000, 0x0000          /* dummy */
        .byte   0x0, 0x0, 0x0, 0x0
        .word   0x0000, 0x0000          /* dummy */
        .byte   0x0, 0x0, 0x0, 0x0
        .word   0xffff, 0x0000          /* flat code segment */
        .byte   0x0, 0x9a, 0xcf, 0x0
        .word   0xffff, 0x0000          /* flat data segment */
        .byte   0x0, 0x92, 0xcf, 0x0
        .word   0x0000, 0x0000          /* kernel tss */
        .byte   0x0, 0x0, 0x0, 0x0
```

The next few instructions set up the %es register, invalidate the Translation Lookaside
Buffer, and set the Global Descriptor Table Register to the table defined above:

```
_realstart:
        cli
        movw    %cs, %ax
        movw    %ax, %es
        xor     %eax, %eax
        mov     %eax, %cr3              /* Invalidate TLB*/
        lgdt    gdtptr                 /* load gdt */
```

Next, numerous bits in Control Register zero (%cr0) are set and cleared:

```
        movl    %cr0, %eax
        andl    $0x7FFAFFD1, %eax      /* PG,AM,WP,NE,TS,EM,MP = 0 */
        orl     $0x60000001, %eax      /* CD, NW, PE = 1 */
        movl    %eax, %cr0
```

Now the cache is invalidated using the invd instruction, and then we jump to 32-bit
mode. Note that the jump is just to the next instruction, but the processor changes
from 16-bit to 32-bit during the jump. The first thing we do in 32-bit mode is execute the intel_chip_post_macro(0x10) macro. This macro outputs the argument (0x10
in this case) to port 0x80 for debugging.

```
        invd                           /* invalidate the cache */
        data32
        ljmp    $0x10, $.Lprotected
        .align  4                      /* Be sure prefetch cache reloads */
.Lprotected:
        .code32                        /* We are now in protected mode */
        intel_chip_post_macro(0x10)    /* post 10 */
```

Now we set up the segment registers and stack pointer:

```
movw    $0x18, %ax
movw    %ax, %ds
movw    %ax, %es
movw    %ax, %ss
movw    %ax, %fs                        /* 586 */
movw    %ax, %gs                        /* 586 */
movl    $_PDATABASE, %esp
```

After setting up the stack, the RAM modules are set up using a long sequence of assembly macros that set up the SIS630 directly, using x86 outb instructions. (To save space, they're not shown here; see the LinuxBIOS project itself for further details.)

```
    /* initialize the RAM (different for each motherboard) */
#include "intel_sis630ram.S"
```

Once the RAM chips on the motherboard are set up, the contents of the _data segment are moved from ROM to the _ldata address in RAM:

```
/*
 *      Copy data into RAM and clear the BSS. Since these segments
 *      aren't really that big, we just copy/clear using bytes, not
 *      double words.
 */
        intel_chip_post_macro(0x11)         /* post 11 */

        cld                                 /* clear direction flag */

        /* copy data segment from FLASH ROM to RAM */
        leal    EXT(_ldata), %esi
        leal    EXT(_data), %edi
        movl    $EXT(_eldata), %ecx
        subl    %esi, %ecx
        jz      .Lnodata                    /* should not happen */
        rep
        movsb
.Lnodata:
        intel_chip_post_macro(0x12)         /* post 12 */
```

Next, the stack and BSS area (uninitialized data area) are zeroed out:

```
        /** clear stack */
        xorl    %edi, %edi
        movl    $_PDATABASE, %ecx
        xorl    %eax, %eax
        rep
        stosb

        /** clear bss */
        leal    EXT(_bss), %edi
        movl    $EXT(_ebss), %ecx
        subl    %edi, %ecx
        jz      .Lnobss
```

```
        xorl     %eax, %eax
        rep
        stosb
.Lnobss:
```

We're almost finished with assembly. Memory is up, data is copied, and stack and BSS are clear. Now we call `intel_main()` in C (much easier) and let it do the rest:

```
        intel_chip_post_macro(0xfe)     /* post fe */
        movl     $_PDATABASE, %esp      /* set new stack */
        call     EXT(intel_main)
.Lhlt:  hlt                             /*NOTREACHED*/
        jmp      .Lhlt
```

The `intel_main()` function in `chip/intel/intel_main.c` does most of the work of getting the hardware ready for the operating system, as shown in Listing 4.2. (We don't follow any of the subroutines; that's left to the reader.)

Listing 4.2   **The *intel_main()* Function**

```
/* intel_main.c */
#define LINUXBIOS

extern void linuxbiosmain(unsigned long membase, unsigned long totalram);
extern void malloc_init(unsigned long start, unsigned long end);

void intel_main()
{
    unsigned long totalram = 0;

    intel_post(0x40);
    displayinit();                          // Initialize the display

    malloc_init(0x30000, 0x70000);          // segs 3-6 for malloc'd memory
    printk("Reached intel_main().\n");
    intel_post(0x42);

    // This is a cheap way to buy some performance:
    // Turn cache on the first 2M so that the next few steps
    // are cached
    intel_cache_on(0, 2048);

    intel_post(0x43);

    // Pick how to scan the bus.
    // This is first so we can get at memory size.
    pci_set_method();
    intel_post(0x5f);
    pci_enumerate();
    intel_post(0x66);
```

continues

Listing 4.2 **Continued**

```
// The framebuffer can change how much memory you have.
// So you really need to run this before you size ram.
intel_framebuffer_on();

totalram = sizeram();
intel_post(0x70);
printk("totalram: %ldM\n", totalram/1024);

// Can't size just yet ...
// Mainboard totalram sizing may not be up yet. If it is not ready,
// take a default of 64M
if (!totalram)
        totalram = 64 * 1024;

// Turn on cache before configuring the bus.
printk("Enabling cache...");
intel_cache_on(0, totalram);
intel_post(0x80);
printk("done.\n");
printk("Allocating PCI resources...\n");

// Now do the real bus.
// We round the total ram up a lot for things like the SISFB, which
// shares high memory with the CPU.
//configure_pci(round(totalram, 64 * 1024 * 1024), 0x1000);
pci_configure();
intel_post(0x88);
pci_enable();
intel_post(0x90);
printk("done.\n");

intel_mainboard_fixup();                    // generic mainboard fixup

printk("Enabling extended BIOS access...");
intel_nvram_on();
printk("done.\n");

intel_pci_list();

intel_display_cpuid();
intel_mtrr_check();

intel_keyboard_on();

enable_floppy();

intel_zero_irq_settings();
intel_check_irq_routing_table();
intel_copy_irq_routing_table();
```

```
        printk("Enabling interrupts...");
        intel_interrupts_on();
        printk("done.\n");

        printk("Jumping to linuxbiosmain()...");
        intel_post(0xed);
        linuxbiosmain(0, totalram);
    }
```

The last act of intel_main() is to call linuxbiosmain(). Up to now, the code has done things that any BIOS would do. The linuxbiosmain() function is really the OS loader—it's going to load the operating system from NVRAM. Listing 4.3 is adapted from linuxbiosmain(). Again, we don't follow the subroutines (such as gunzip()).

Listing 4.3   **Loading the Operating System from NVRAM**

```
int
    linuxbiosmain(unsigned long base, unsigned long totalram)
    {
        unsigned char *empty_zero_page;

        printk("Welcome to start32, the open sourced starter.\n");
        printk("This space will eventually hold more diagnostic info.\n");
        printk("\n");
        printk("James Hendricks, Dale Webster, and Ron Minnich.\n");
        printk("Version 0.1\n");
        printk("\n");

        setup_output_buffer();

        DBG("Making CRC\n");
        makecrc();
        intel_post(0xf1);

        DBG("Gunzipping boot code\n");
        if (gunzip() != 0) {
            printk("gunzip failed\n");
            intel_post(0xff);
              return 0;
        }
        intel_post(0xf8);

        /* Parameter passing to Linux. You have to get the pointer to the
         * empty_zero_page, then fill it in.
         */
        empty_zero_page = get_empty_zero_page();
        init_params(empty_zero_page);
        intel_post(0xf9);
```

continues

Listing 4.3 **Continued**

```
                /* The ram address should be the last mbyte, AFAIK. Subtract one for
                 * the low 1 MB. So subtract 2K total.
                 */
                set_memory_size(empty_zero_page, 0x3c00, totalram - 2048);
                intel_post(0xfa);
                DBG("using command line - [%s]\n", CMD_LINE);

                set_command_line(empty_zero_page, CMD_LINE);
                set_root_rdonly(empty_zero_page);
                set_display(empty_zero_page, 25, 80);

                /* set up the IO-APIC for the clock interrupt. */
                setup_apic();
                intel_post(0xfc);

                DBG("Jumping to boot code\n");
                intel_post(0xfe);

                /* Move 0x90000 to into esi. (This is the addr of the linux parm page.)
                 * Linux then copies this page into its "empty_zero_page" so it isn't
                 * stomped while things are being set up.
                 * Later the "empty_zero_page" is zeroed and used to fulfill read
                 * demands on memory mappings of file holes and the like.
                 * As of 2.4.0-test4 the Linux parameter page isn't hardwired to be
                 * at 0x90000 anymore.
                 */
                /* Move 0 to ebx. This is for SMP support. Jump to kernel */
                __asm__ __volatile__("movl $0x90000, %%esi\n\t"
                                     "movl $0, %%ebx\n\t"
                                     "ljmp $0x10, %0\n\t"
                                     :: "i" (0x100000));
                return 0;                      /* It should never return */
        }
```

The `ljmp` instruction above jumps into the real Linux kernel in NVRAM. All of this code takes very little time to execute.

Linux Kernel

When you compile Linux using the `make` command, one of the last `ld` commands builds the kernel file (`vmlinux`) itself:

```
ld -m elf_i386 -T /usr/src/linux/arch/i386/vmlinux.lds
⮡      -e stext arch/i386/kernel/head.o arch/i386/kernel/init_task.o
⮡      init/main.o init/version.o \
            --start-group \
            arch/i386/kernel/kernel.o arch/i386/mm/mm.o
⮡         kernel/kernel.o mm/mm.o fs/fs.o ipc/ipc.o \
            fs/filesystems.a \
```

```
             net/network.a \
             drivers/block/block.a drivers/char/char.a
➥                      drivers/misc/misc.a drivers/net/net.a
➥                      drivers/cdrom/cdrom.a drivers/pci/pci.a
➥                      drivers/video/video.a arch/i386/math-emu/math.a \
             /usr/src/linux/arch/i386/lib/lib.a
➥                      /usr/src/linux/lib/lib.a
➥                      /usr/src/linux/arch/i386/lib/lib.a \
         --end-group \
         -o vmlinux
```

Part of the `ld` command is the `-T /usr/src/linux/arch/i386/vmlinux.lds` option. This option causes the `ld` command to throw away all of its defaults and use the referenced `.lds` file to discover its link format. Part of the `vmlinux.lds.S` (the source to `vmlinux.lds`) is shown in the following listing. Notice the line that reads `. = PAGE_OFFSET_RAW + 0x100000;`. This tells `ld` that the `.text` section should start at location `PAGE_OFFSET_RAW + 0x100000`. This matches with the `0x100000` from the `ljmp` instruction at the end of `linuxbiosmain()`.

Also note the `-e stext` option from the `ld` command from the Makefile above—we'll see this in the `arch/i386/kernel/head.S` file within the kernel in a minute.

```
/* ld script to make i386 Linux kernel
 * Written by Martin Mares
 */
OUTPUT_FORMAT("elf32-i386", "elf32-i386", "elf32-i386")
OUTPUT_ARCH(i386)
ENTRY(_start)
SECTIONS
{
  . = PAGE_OFFSET_RAW + 0x100000;
  _text = .;                      /* Text and read-only data */
  .text : {
        *(.text)
        *(.fixup)
        *(.gnu.warning)
        } = 0x9090

  ...

}
```

The Linux kernel starts in a bit of assembly code within a file called `head.S`. The following listing is adapted from the i386 architecture tree. Remember the `stext` label from the `-e` option of the `ld` command? It's the first label in the `head.S` assembly source file.

```
/* linux/arch/i386/head.S -- the 32-bit startup code.
 * Copyright (C) 1991, 1992  Linus Torvalds
 */

.text
```

continues

Continued

```
ENTRY(stext)
ENTRY(_stext)
startup_32:
/* Set segments to known values */
        cld
        movl $(__KERNEL_DS),%eax
        movl %ax,%ds
        movl %ax,%es
...
```

Note that a lot of code is skipped here. If you really want to get a good idea of how Linux boots, head.S is a good place to start.

Once the fair bit of assembly code in head.S is done, the start_kernel() function is called. Notice that the start_kernel() function should never return, or the kernel will go into an infinite loop, starting at the L6 label.

```
lss stack_start,%esp     # Load processor stack
        xorl %eax,%eax
        lldt %ax
        cld                  # gcc2 wants the direction flag cleared at all times
        call SYMBOL_NAME(start_kernel)
L6:
        jmp L6               # main should never return here, but
                             # just in case, we know what happens.

#ifdef __SMP__
ready:  .byte 0
#endif
```

The start_kernel() function in init/main.c is the first non–machine-specific Linux code that runs. The first thing it does is print the Linux banner; then it starts initializing all the various parts of the kernel.

Note that lots of code from the start_kernel() function (shown in Listing 4.4) has been stripped for brevity.

Listing 4.4 **The *start_kernel()* Function**

```
/*  linux/init/main.c
 *  Copyright (C) 1991, 1992  Linus Torvalds
 */

...a lot of code skipped here...

asmlinkage void __init start_kernel(void)
{
        char * command_line;

        printk(linux_banner);
        setup_arch(&command_line, &memory_start, &memory_end);
        memory_start = paging_init(memory_start,memory_end);
        trap_init();
```

```
memory_start = init_IRQ( memory_start );
sched_init();
time_init();
parse_options(command_line);
memory_start = console_init(memory_start,memory_end);
init_modules();
memory_start = kmem_cache_init(memory_start, memory_end);
sti();
calibrate_delay();
mem_init(memory_start,memory_end);
kmem_cache_sizes_init();
proc_root_init();
uidcache_init();
filescache_init();
dcache_init();
vma_init();
buffer_init(memory_end-memory_start);
page_cache_init(memory_end-memory_start);
signals_init();
inode_init();
file_table_init();
check_bugs();
printk("POSIX conformance testing by UNIFIX\n");

/*
 *      We count on the initial thread going ok.
 *      Like idlers init is an unlocked kernel thread, which will
 *      make syscalls (and thus be locked).
 */
smp_init();
kernel_thread(init, NULL, CLONE_FS | CLONE_FILES | CLONE_SIGHAND);
current->need_resched = 1;
cpu_idle(NULL);
}
```

Summary

Conceptually, booting the Linux kernel is not all that difficult. You need some sort of "BIOS" that does the really low-level startup stuff. When the BIOS is done, it runs the OS loader, which loads the OS from the boot media and jumps into it. The OS then has control of the computer and continues bringing itself up.

II

Hardware

5

Hardware Considerations

Previous chapters examined the many issues and advantages related to using Linux in embedded environments. Of course, the eventual goal is an actual physical product, and that means *hardware*. If you were creating a Linux application to run on a standard PC, your task would be greatly simplified, because the environment is well defined and doesn't vary much from one manufacturer to another. But because the embedded world includes a huge number of different product types and requirements, that means an equal number of potential hardware solutions and difficult decisions to be made. Unfortunately, the perfect hardware solution for the motorized hula-hoop controller you have in mind is probably *not* going to be the perfect solution for the nuclear-powered, telepathically controlled, handheld inertial navigation system that your boss wants you to build.

There simply is *no* universal platform that fits all needs. That's the bad news.

The good news is that Linux support is available for virtually every microprocessor type and family in existence, from simple micro-controllers that cost only a few dollars to sophisticated multiprocessor systems with supercomputer performance and hefty price tags. Whatever your application, it's certain that one or more appropriate choices are available. And, while there is no simple cookbook method for instantly selecting the right hardware solution, you can apply some well-known guidelines to make the process manageable.

Determining the Design Goal

The overall goal for any embedded designer can be summed up quite easily:
Better, faster, cheaper.

- *Better* in the sense that you choose a high-quality hardware solution that perfectly matches the system requirements with the minimal number of components and with excess horsepower for the inevitable feature-creep that any product faces during development. The ideal choice would include all necessary memory and peripheral functions onboard, occupy minimal space, and consume almost no power.

- *Faster* by bringing the product to market in the least amount of time possible, preferably before your competition even knows the work has begun.

- *Cheaper* for the obvious reasons—the lower the cost to the customer, the higher the volume. The higher the volume, the more profit per engineering dollar spent.

Of course, reality dictates that not all of these goals can be achieved simultaneously, as the experienced designer knows. In fact, satisfying any two of these goals represents a remarkable accomplishment and is the practical upper limit. Therefore, your first and most essential task is to select the *one* main objective that is the ultimate aim of your project: better? faster? or cheaper? This information helps drive all subsequent processes because it forces you to focus on what's important. If you're trying to beat the competition to market, you need to work fast; you can give up some cost advantages by using off-the-shelf parts instead of engineering and building your own. However, if you're designing a system that will control equipment that can endanger human life, your overriding concern is quality; you'll take the time necessary to ensure quality, and spend the money on higher-quality parts. If you need to build the least expensive box possible because your quantities are immense, you'll spend the time engineering the box and live with tradeoffs on quality.

Buy or Build?

Long before the decision is made to fire up the CAD workstation and begin capturing schematics, you should take the time to do a thorough search of existing products and components to see whether what you need already exists. After all, you're creating this new widget because there's a glaring and obvious need, right? In other words, a real market? If the market exists, it's likely that other people have recognized that fact and will already be offering "solutions" of one sort or another—even though their solutions might be inferior to what *you* have in mind. But perhaps you could adapt, rework, enhance, or otherwise improve upon what's already out there.

While you're doing this research, don't be afraid to approach potential competitors. You may find that they would be more than willing to defray some of their own development and manufacturing costs by selling you a hardware platform to which you can add your own differentiating features via software. This scenario is particularly likely with offshore manufacturers, who may not have your marketing or distribution expertise or home field sales advantage.

As a general rule, unless you intend to build minimum quantities of several thousand per month or your requirement is so unique that there's *no* possibility of economically using anything off the shelf, you should shop for screwdrivers instead of CAD tools. If you do decide to buy rather than build, don't be disappointed at having to suppress the engineer's natural instinct to invent. There will still be plenty of other opportunities for challenge and excitement (like it or not).

The "Cheap PC" Myth

Inevitably, while you're researching platform possibilities, someone (most likely from Operations or Administration) will feel compelled to deliver an impassioned lecture that goes into exquisite detail in pointing out the galactically obvious: *Desktop PCs are ubiquitous, powerful, and incredibly cheap.* It follows from this argument that if you could simply develop your product based on an ordinary PC, then it too would become ubiquitous, powerful, and (in lieu of cheap) immensely profitable.

In fact, there are a great many valid and compelling arguments that *can* be made for adopting such a strategy, including reduced development time, expense, and risk. However, you can't safely assume that you will get the same cost savings as the large PC OEMs. While you may use the same basic components (processor, chipset, memory), and these are produced in tremendous cost-reducing volumes, realistically they represent only a small fraction of the completed system cost. If you really can use standard, unmodified PC components, you may save some money. But if you need a different form-factor or user interface, diskless operation, alternative power sources, or any other modifications, your "standard PC" starts looking more and more like a wide range of other alternatives.

One closely related alternative involves the use of so-called "industrial PCs," which utilize standard form-factor boards with a passive ISA or PCI backplane in a rugged (typically rack-mounted) enclosure. If you've already done some shopping for these industrial PC components, you're well aware of the huge cost difference between that PC you purchased at a discount warehouse for development use and its equivalent (or lesser) industrial version. The industrial version can easily cost three to four times as much for the same functionality. Many developers aren't aware of this difference until they've committed the project to being PC-compatible, and then it's too late to reverse the decision easily. This makes the industrial PC suppliers very happy.

The alternative to using an industrial product, which ostensibly offers great long-term availability and reliability, is to settle for the "motherboard du jour" approach. Under this system, you use whatever boards are available; although these boards may indeed be PC-compatible (by definition), some will also be completely different in terms of component layout, heat distribution, core chipsets, BIOS features, power requirements, memory compatibility, processor vendors, peripheral functions, mechanical mounting, and cabling/connector requirements. The PC industry is evolving so rapidly and the competitive cost pressures are so great that in many cases the manufacturer will initiate a complete redesign to save only a few *cents* per board. As a result, the use of "standard motherboards" means that your product will be subject to constant change and evolution completely beyond your control. This is guaranteed to have some undesirable consequences, despite any "compatibility" claims.

Perhaps you have other reasons for wanting a PC-compatible platform, such as the ability to reuse existing code, legacy applications or hardware interfaces, or specialized development tools. At the same time, you may find that the industrial approach is either too expensive or doesn't offer the flexibility or feature set that you need. In this case, you have the option of designing your own "motherboard."

The major silicon vendors continue to devise new variations of x86-family processors and chipsets targeted for embedded applications. More importantly, they're finally beginning to address the need for a stable and long-term supply chain for both the processors and companion chipsets that's more in line with the expected lifecycles of the products in which they'll be used. What's more, some manufacturers are willing to simplify the design process by supplying a wealth of reference materials, evaluation systems, and even complete ready-to-use designs in CAD format. All you have to do is ask—but be prepared to "do the math" anyway, since you still have to contend with PCB layouts, mechanical and thermal issues, assembly and test, EMI and safety, and a wide range of other issues that apply to any product—whether PC-compatible or not.

If it sounds as though I'm discouraging the use of PCs for embedded Linux, rest assured that I'm not. It's just that there are many alternatives in addition to the standard PC that are often neglected because the "PC option" seems so obvious. Still, the PC approach can be, and often is, the best fit.

Another, more expensive approach is to use notebook components. These tend to be rugged and small. You can take the main-logic board and mount it in a new box. Besides being rugged, many logic boards have built-in power supplies and charging circuits.

SBCs and Other Options

Pursuing the "buy" option? There are quite a few alternatives to desktop or industrial PCs. These generally fall into two categories: *single-board computers* (*SBCs*) with little or no expansion capability beyond the features provided onboard, or modular systems products based on specific bus standards.

Single-board computers come in a wide range of standard and custom form-factors. The most common types usually have a mechanical footprint equivalent to either a 3 1/2-inch disk drive or the slightly larger CD-ROM drive size. Most are PC compatible, although it's not uncommon to find other processor families supported as well (for example, PowerPC or StrongARM).

SBCs also tend to cost slightly less than the industrial-PC products, but be aware that the reduced cost comes at the expense of having limited expansion capability. As a result, SBC designers tend to take a "kitchen sink" approach by including as many peripheral functions as they can possibly squeeze onto a relatively small PCB, often using nonstandard connectors to save additional space. Power requirements vary wildly depending on processor type, speed grade, type of memory used, and peripheral functions available.

If you're lucky enough to find an SBC that offers the exact mix of performance and functionality you need, you still have to contend with packaging it and a power supply, along with anything else you need (display, controls, cooling, and so forth) in a suitable enclosure. In my experience, the small form-factor usually provides little bene-fit once the other bits and pieces are added and the myriad cable and connector issues are sorted out.

Perhaps the biggest drawback of SBCs is the limited expansion capability. It never seems to fail that the one interface you need—typically the thing that makes your application and product unique—is not available and will require substantial thrashing and contortions on your part to accommodate and adapt.

And finally there's the cost. If you're building one or a small number of something truly custom (in other words, not intended for ongoing production), the cost savings of using the SBC will disappear once the other costs (assembly, configuration, docu-mentation, and so on) are assimilated.

A somewhat more flexible approach is provided by a number of bus-based prod-ucts, including PC104 and PC104+, STD bus, VME bus, CompactPCI, and others, all of which conform to published standards and are supported by extensive supplier organizations. The cost of these products is usually on par with the industrial-PC equivalents, but in many cases they can cost considerably more. The benefits include much greater flexibility in packaging, processor/performance options, increased supplier base, and—theoretically, at least—choice of off-the-shelf interface types and functions.

The primary advantage to be derived from using any of these systems is that it allows you to build custom functions to be added according to well-defined standards in a well-known, documented environment. But notice that I said *build*—meaning that you have already determined that some elements of your product will have to be engineered, designed, and constructed by you. What's more, you've also determined that your performance or throughput requirements demand this level of sophistication. This approach, a combination of "buy" and "build," represents the top of the food chain as far as *embedded* is defined. Systems like these are typically embedded in airliners, oil tankers, and skyscrapers—not wristwatches. Yet Linux can be equally at home in all of these cases.

Custom Design

If your search for a ready-made hardware platform fails to turn up anything promising or suitable, or if your volume and cost requirements warrant going into full production, you may have no choice but to design it yourself. Obviously, this approach yields the utmost in flexibility but provides the greatest risk as well as many challenges. You can design the hardware yourself if you have the in-house talent, or you can hire a consultant to do the designing.

Processor Choices

Because Linux has been ported to virtually every processor type and family, it's unlikely that you'll have to start from scratch and do all the work yourself. This also means that the available choices in terms of performance, cost, power consumption, and peripheral functions are nearly unlimited, and you won't be forced to make giant compromises just to accommodate some obscure processor family.

It's very important to do your homework on the processor you choose. For instance, it's much easier to work with a processor that has a *memory management unit* (*MMU*) than a processor without one. A memory management unit provides differentiated address spaces for the kernel and each process, enforces memory protection, and provides for virtual memory. Without an MMU, these desirable features simply don't exist.

The uClinux kernel fork was created specifically so you can use the MMU-less processors, but your application programs must behave quite differently when running in an MMU-less environment. For instance, because you can change any part of memory, including kernel memory, it's quite easy for your application to completely freeze an MMU-less processor.

Storage Choices and Memory Requirements

Perhaps the biggest concern to be addressed concerns memory requirements—type, amount, and partitioning. Linux will probably never be as compact as some of the commercially available embedded OS products, but that's the price to be paid for obtaining the power and flexibility that Linux offers. Besides, these days product costs continue to decline even as memory and storage capacities increase.

Typical embedded Linux products are partitioned very much like their desktop counterparts, in that there is usually a small amount of dedicated boot and configuration memory (BIOS), an area of main memory and solid-state storage that replaces the usual disk drive. Because of its UNIX heritage, the simplest way to adapt Linux is to retain a disk-like device and file structure. The most common way this is accomplished is to use flash memory, which emulates a drive—for example, the DiskOnChip or CompactFlash devices, which provide an IDE interface.

Input/Output

There are as many choices for I/O devices as there are embedded systems. Your application will determine what type of I/O devices you need. Fortunately, a veritable army of Linux programmers have had years to develop and refine the necessary device drivers to support nearly any hardware imaginable. Probably the best example can be seen in the large number of network controllers supported. Chances are good that if a peripheral function exists on silicon, someone has already written the supporting code. Significantly, this includes the component manufacturers themselves, as Linux has become a major force in the marketplace in recent years.

If your requirements are very simple (for example, a few LEDs and simple switches), chances are good that you can use a low-cost parallel port by slightly modifying the drivers. Some very simple systems require no I/O at all. While a device with no I/O probably wouldn't be very useful, such devices are possible, since Linux, unlike Windows, has no set hardware requirements. Therefore, the choice is entirely up to you.

Display

As mentioned previously, Linux doesn't require any particular type or format of display device to be present, but—at least for debugging and development purposes—you probably want to consider some form of display. It need not be very elaborate, often consisting of nothing more than a serial port that can be connected to a PC in terminal mode.

For dedicated displays, which are sometimes required, you can use inexpensive LCD or vacuum fluorescent (VF) displays, which use a common parallel port; various examples and drivers are available. For more sophisticated needs, graphics controllers intended for PCs are readily available and inexpensive.

Summary

Choosing the proper hardware for your embedded Linux device doesn't have to be a nightmare. Choose your overriding design goal: better, faster, or cheaper. Once you've done that, the rest of the questions should be a lot easier. Do you want to buy or build? And exactly what hardware do you want to use?

Implementing an Embedded Linux Application

6

Embedded Linux Toolkits

THE MOST STRAIGHTFORWARD WAY OF EMBEDDING LINUX into the device of your choice is to grab the latest Linux kernel, a cross-compiler for your target hardware, a C library, and some applications—and start hacking. The problem is that you'll spend an awful lot of time hacking before you have something that simply boots, let alone actually does what you want it to do.

In 1999–2000, many people in the Linux community realized how applicable Linux is to a large number of problems in the embedded application space. They also realized how non-trivial it is to create a working Linux system for the typical embedded platform. Many software toolkits were built to simplify the job of creating the software for these embedded Linux devices. Some of these toolkits come from newly created and well-funded companies; others come from companies that have been in the embedded market for quite some time but have decided to reinvent themselves for Linux. Still others don't come from companies at all, but are Open Source projects built up from collaborations across the Internet.

This chapter attempts to make sense of the jumbled mishmash of competing embedded Linux toolkits available as of 2001. Of course, as I write these words, the world continues to spin—so the landscape may be very different as you read this. However, I've attempted to define the questions that you should be asking of the packages you're considering.

What Constitutes an "Embedded Linux Toolkit"?

There are a lot of products and projects available on the Internet that can help you with various aspects of building the software for your embedded Linux device. I'm defining an "embedded Linux toolkit" to include only those products and projects that, together with a host Linux system and the target hardware, provide a complete end-to-end solution for building the image that you load onto the hardware that will boot Linux and run at least a simple application.

Each toolkit has a different user interface and style. However, all must do essentially the same thing: Build a Linux kernel that either contains the application as a kernel thread or also builds a root filesystem with the application software in it. The toolkit must then be able to install the pieces into a binary image from which the target system boots.

For example, by my definition, BusyBox is not an "embedded Linux toolkit." BusyBox is a great piece of technology that shoehorns a lot of software into a very small space; it's especially useful for statically linked environments. But by itself, BusyBox doesn't contain enough software to create a complete Linux system.

This chapter takes a close look at two embedded Linux toolkits:

- BlueCat from LynuxWorks (www.LynuxWorks.com)
- PeeWeeLinux (www.peeweelinux.org)

In addition to these, some of the items in the following list may fill your needs. This is by no means a comprehensive list of toolkits. There are many other products and projects available that you can consider.

- The Embedded Debian Project (www.emdebian.org)
- Embedded DevKit (EDK) and GNUPro Tools from Red Hat (www.redhat.com/embedded)
- Embedix from Lineo (www.lineo.com)
- Hard Hat Linux from MontaVista (www.mvista.com)
- Linux Router Project (www.linuxrouter.org)

Considerations

While you're considering the various toolkits, you should try to answer the following general questions. You should also make up a list of questions specific to your project.

- What is the size of image produced?
- What architectures are supported?
- How easy is the toolkit to use?

- How many optional packages are available?
- What exceptional packages are available? (Web-based administration, perhaps?)
- How customizable is the image? How difficult is it to customize?
- How much does the toolkit cost? Is a royalty involved?
- How well is the toolkit documented? Is printed documentation available?
- How well is the toolkit supported? Paid support? Active list?
- What are the requirements to use the toolkit?
- Can a new version of the toolkit be installed without losing changes?

To test the toolkits, I tried to build a single floppy x86 boot disk that would run the Minicom application (for more on Minicom, see Chapter 8, "Static Application Example: Minicom").

BlueCat Linux from LynuxWorks (*www.LynuxWorks.com*)

LynuxWorks's BlueCat Linux Version 3.0 is a professional embedded Linux toolkit that's fully documented, supports a broad range of target hardware, and is freely downloadable (although you have to agree not to develop commercial applications with the freely downloadable version). The software is distributed on several CDs—one for all of the source code, and one for the binaries of each architecture.

LynuxWorks's CDK includes the following items:

- Compilers for C, C++, and Java
- Hooks for the GDB debugger
- Performance measurement tools
- A small set of network tools and applications

The following target processor families are supported:

- Intel IA-32 (x86)
- PowerPC
- PowerQUICC
- ARM/ARM7/ARM9/StrongARM
- Super-H
- MIPS R3000/R4000

The following host operating systems are supported:

- Red Hat 6.1 and 6.2
- TurboLinux Workstation, version 6.0
- Windows 98/NT/2000

Using BlueCat Linux

I was able to install BlueCat Linux version 3.0 and get my serial communications floppy running in about a day. The documentation is quite good. The following procedure outlines the general steps I followed:

1. Obtain root privileges to your machine.

2. As root, enter the following command to create a `bluecat` directory within `/tmp`:

    ```
    mkdir -p /tmp/bluecat
    ```

    The BlueCat tarball contains multiple files and directories in the root (naughty). By putting all these files into an empty directory in `/tmp`, you can easily delete them after install.

3. Now let's download the `x86-linux.tar.gz` file from the BlueCat Web site with the following command:

    ```
    cd /tmp/bluecat; lynx http://www.LynuxWorks.com/...
    ```

    At 70MB, it will take a bit of time.

4. Extract the archive with the following command:

    ```
    tar xvzf x86-linux.tar.gz
    ```

    When this process is finished, you'll have an `install` script and a `BlueCat_i386` directory.

5. Create the `bluecat` user:

    ```
    adduser bluecat
    ```

    You can put the software somewhere else if you prefer.

6. Change to the `bluecat` user:

    ```
    cd ~bluecat
    ```

7. Create a `bluecat` directory within the `bluecat` user's home directory and `cd` to it:

    ```
    mkdir bluecat ; cd bluecat
    ```

    I tried to install the BlueCat software directly into the `bluecat` user's home directory, but the install script will only install into a directory with no other files. Users' home directories always have lots of hidden junk in them, which will prevent installation, so using a subdirectory is a requirement.

8. Install the BlueCat software with this command:

    ```
    /tmp/bluecat/install
    ```

    When the install completes, you'll have nine new directories and a setup script in the `~bluecat/bluecat` directory. The directories (`bin`, `boot`, `cdt`, `demo.x86`, `etc`, `lib`, `sbin`, `usr`, and `var`) contain, among other things, the cross-compiler tools and the target's executables. Of course, for this demonstration, both the build environment and the target are x86, so it's not really cross-compiling, but you get the point.

9. Source the `SETUP.sh` script into your current shell using the dot command:

    `. SETUP.sh`

    This script sets up several environment variables to work with BlueCat. It also updates your `PATH` to include the paths to the BlueCat build tools and updates your `MANPATH` so that you can view the BlueCat man pages. Finally, this script adds `Bluecat:` to the beginning of your command prompt so you know you're in "BlueCat" mode.

10. Change to the `demo` directory:

    `cd demo`

    BlueCat creates a symbolic link named `demo` that points to the `demo.x86` directory. Within the `demo` directory are seven different demo projects: `default`, `disk`, `hello`, `osloader`, `ping`, `shell`, and `tcl`.

11. Make a copy of the `shell` demo and call it `minicom`:

    `cp -r shell minicom`

12. Change to the `minicom` directory:

    `cd minicom`

13. The shell demo came with a `shell.config` file. Since our example is called `minicom`, we must rename `shell.config` to `minicom.config`:

    `mv shell.config minicom.config`

14. For the same reason, rename `shell.spec` to `minicom.spec`:

    `mv shell.spec minicom.spec`

15. Make a new directory called `minicom`:

    `mkdir minicom`

    We'll keep the source files for Minicom here.

16. Change to the new `minicom` directory:

    `cd minicom`

17. Download Minicom from `http://www.pp.clinet.fi/~walker/minicom.html`.

    If it's not there, try `http://www.freshmeat.net` to find it. If you have trouble downloading it, use `http://ftpsearch.lycos.com` to search for the filename, and then pick a site near you to download from. At the time of this writing, the latest version was 1.83.1.

18. Untar Minicom (if you want to see the files that are created, type `xvzf` instead of `xzf`):

    `tar xzf minicom-1.83.1.src.tar.gz`

19. Create a symbolic link named `minicom` that points to `minicom-1.83.1`:

    `ln -s minicom-1.83.1 minicom`

    This symbolic link will be used in the `opt/minicom/Makefile`; if you decide to upgrade to a later version of Minicom in the future, you can just change the symbolic link to point to the new one.

20. We have to make a small change to the Minicom source code to make sure that it works properly in our mini-environment. Change to the `minicom` source directory:

    ```
    cd minicom/src
    ```

21. Let's remove a Minicom security feature that's unnecessary in an embedded application. In `minicom.c`, search for the following line:

    ```
    if (real_uid == 0 && dosetup == 0) {
    ```

    Delete about 61 lines—up to, but not including this line:

    ```
    buf[0] = 0;
    ```

    If these lines are not removed, Minicom will bail out at this point. Since we don't have to be concerned with permissions and correct users in our embedded environment, it's safe to just skip this code.

22. Save your changes.

23. BlueCat comes with all of its own libraries for the target environment, but the free version doesn't come with the `ncurses` library installed, so we're going to cheat a bit:

    ```
    vi Makefile
    ```

    Search for the following line within a group of assignments that say we're compiling for Linux with `libncurses`:

    ```
    LIBS = -lncurses #-lintl
    ```

    Change the line to read as follows:

    ```
    LIBS = -L /usr/lib -lncurses #-lintl
    ```

    We could have downloaded the `ncurses` library from the Internet and built it using the BlueCat build tools in a separate directory, then linked with it. If you're building a real embedded device, that's exactly what you *should* do. But that procedure takes a dozen more steps and adds little to the book, so instead I'm showing you how to take advantage of the fact that our host environment is the same as our target environment; we can just use the `ncurses` library that's installed with the host environment. This is handy if you want to kludge something up for testing (as long as you remember to fix it later).

24. Back to Makefile:

    ```
    vi Makefile
    ```

    Find the following line:

    ```
    minicom: $(MOBJS)
    ```

    Insert the text `-static` before the text `-o minicom` on the next line. We need to make the `minicom` executable static because BlueCat won't use the shared `ncurses` library from the host machine.

25. Now make the `minicom` executable file:

    ```
    make
    ```

In a real project, you would modify the project Makefile to make `minicom` instead of building the executable "by hand" in this directory.

26. Okay, back to the root of our project:

```
cd ../../..
```

27. Ready for another Makefile change?

```
vi Makefile
```

Find the third line:

```
KDI_NAME = shell
```

Change it to read as follows:

```
KDI_NAME = minicom
```

28. Another ncurses kludge. This one is fairly harmless since this file is architecture-independent. Minicom needs the `terminfo` file for the Linux console "terminal" type:

```
cp /usr/share/terminfo/l/linux local
```

29. Now we need to make some changes to the `minicom.spec` file:

```
vi minicom.spec
```

Here's the first line:

```
# shell.spec
```

Change it to read as follows:

```
# minicom.spec
```

It's just a comment, but you might as well fix it. Now find the following line:

```
ln -s /dev/console /dev/tty1
```

Add the following lines after it:

```
mknod /dev/ttyS0 c 4 64
mknod /dev/ttyS1 c 4 65
mknod /dev/ttyS2 c 4 66
mknod /dev/ttyS3 c 4 67
```

These lines create the device nodes for the four serial ports on the target system's `/dev` directory.

Now find the following line:

```
mkdir -p /var/run
```

Add the following line after it (note that the last character is the lowercase letter *L*):

```
mkdir -p /usr/share/terminfo/l
```

This creates the directory for the `terminfo` file.

Almost there. Find this line:

```
cp ./local/rc.sysinit /etc/rc.d
```

Add the following lines after it:

```
cp ./local/linux /usr/share/terminfo/l
cp ./minicom/minicom/src/minicom /bin
```

These lines put the `minicom` executable and the `terminfo` file onto the target's root filesystem.

30. Now we need to edit the file. Run the `vi` command:

```
vi local/inittab
```

The last line should look like this:

```
1:12345:respawn:/sbin/mingetty tty1
```

Change the line to read as follows:

```
1:12345:respawn:/bin/minicom
```

Be sure to take the `s` out of `sbin`. This forces the `init` program to run the `minicom` command when it's done initializing the machine.

31. Run the `make` command to make the BlueCat project:

```
make
```

The first time through it has to rebuild the kernel, so it'll take a while.

32. Now create the boot floppy:

```
mkboot -b -k minicom.disk -f minicom.rfs -r /dev/fd0 /dev/fd0
```

The `mkboot` command is part of the BlueCat distribution. It creates a bootable image on the specified device (`/dev/fd0`) from the parts created by the `make` command. The `minicom.disk` file is a copy of `bzImage` from the kernel in `~bluecat/bluecat/usr/src/linux`. The `minicom.rfs` file was built by BlueCat's `mkrootfs` command during the `make`. One problem with the `mkboot` command is that it must output to a real device if you use the `-b` option. This is a problem if you use hardware emulation software such as VMware and never actually create a real floppy disk. For example, while testing BlueCat, I had to build a real floppy disk with the `mkboot` command and then use the `dd` command to pull the image back off the floppy and send it to a file.

33. Boot the floppy disk on your target device. With a little luck, trusty old Minicom should appear for your serial terminal needs.

What's Included with BlueCat Linux?

More than 20 packages are included in the base BlueCat Linux distribution:

Package	Version	License	Description
SysVinit_trg	2.77-1	GPL	The SysVinit package contains a group of processes that control the very basic functions of your system. SysVinit includes the `init` program, the first program started by the Linux

Package	Version	License	Description
			kernel when the system boots. `init` then controls the startup, running, and shutdown of all other programs.
bash_trg	1.14.7-1	GPL	`bash` is a GNU project `sh`-compatible shell or command language interpreter. `bash` (short for Bourne again shell) incorporates useful features from the Korn shell (`ksh`) and the C shell (`csh`). Most `sh` scripts can be run by `bash` without modification.
			`bash` offers several improvements over `sh`, including command-line editing, unlimited-size command history, job control, shell functions and aliases, indexed arrays of unlimited size, and integer arithmetic in any base from 2 to 64. `bash` is ultimately intended to conform to the IEEE POSIX P1003.2/ISO 9945.2 Shell and Tools standard.
			`bash` is the default shell for Red Hat Linux. You should install `bash` because of its popularity and power. You'll probably end up using it.
demo_trg-x86	1.0-1	LynuxWorks	This RPM contains all BlueCat Linux demo configurations.
e2fsprogs_trg	1.15-1	GPL	The `e2fsprogs` package contains a number of utilities for creating, checking, modifying, and correcting any inconsistencies in second extended (ext2) filesystems. `e2fsprogs` contains `e2fsck` (used to repair filesystem inconsistencies after an unclean shutdown), `mke2fs` (used to initialize a partition to contain an empty ext2 filesystem), `debugfs` (used to examine the internal structure of a filesystem, to manually repair a corrupted filesystem, or to create test cases for `e2fsck`), `tune2fs` (used to modify filesystem parameters), and most of the other core ext2fs filesystem utilities.

continues

Package	Version	License	Description
			You should install the e2fsprogs package if you need to manage the performance of an ext2 filesystem.
ffs_trg	1.0-1	LynuxWorks	BlueCat Linux Flash File System provides a filesystem directly on Flash, rather than emulating a block device. FFS is intended to provide a crash/powerdown-safe filesystem for diskless embedded devices.
fileutils_trg	4.0-1	GPL	The fileutils package includes a number of GNU versions of common and popular file-management utilities. fileutils includes the following tools: chgrp (changes a file's group ownership), chown (changes a file's ownership), chmod (changes a file's permissions), cp (copies files), dd (copies and converts files), df (shows a filesystem's disk usage), dir (gives a brief directory listing), dircolors (the setup program for the color version of the ls command), du (shows disk usage), install (copies files and sets permissions), ln (creates file links), ls (lists directory contents), mkdir (creates directories), mkfifo (creates FIFOs or named pipes), mknod (creates special files), mv (renames files), rm (removes/deletes files), rmdir (removes empty directories), sync (synchronizes memory and disk), touch (changes file timestamps), and vdir (provides long directory listings).
			You should install the fileutils package because it includes many file-management utilities that you'll use frequently.
glibc_trg	2.1.2-1 L	GPL	The glibc package contains standard libraries that are used by multiple programs on the system. To save disk space and memory, as well as make upgrading easier, common system code is kept in one place and shared

Package	Version	License	Description
			between programs. This particular package contains the most important sets of shared libraries: the standard C library and the standard math library. Without these two libraries, a Linux system won't function. The `glibc` package also contains national language (locale) support and timezone databases.
glibc_trg-devel	2.1.2-1	LGPL	The `glibc-devel` package contains the header and object files necessary for developing programs that use the standard C libraries (which are used by nearly all programs). If you're developing programs that will use the standard C libraries, your system needs to have these standard header and object files available in order to create the executables.
			Install `glibc-devel` if you're going to develop programs that will use the standard C libraries.
kernel_trg-bcboot	2.2.12-1	GPL	This package contains the BlueCat boot sector used by installation tools to make hard disks and floppies bootable with the BlueCat kernel.
kernel_trg-headers	2.2.12-1	GPL	`kernel-headers` includes the C header files for the Linux kernel. The header files define structures and constants that are needed for building most standard programs and are also needed for rebuilding the kernel.
kernel_trg-source	2.2.12-1	GPL	The `kernel-source` package contains the source code files for the Linux kernel. These source files are needed to build most C programs, since they depend on the constants defined in the source code. The source files can also be used to build a custom kernel that is better tuned to your particular hardware, if you are so inclined (and you know what you're doing).

continues

Package	Version	License	Description
kernel_trg-x86	2.2.12-1	GPL	The kernel package contains the Linux kernel (vmlinuz), the core of your Red Hat Linux operating system. The kernel handles the basic functions of the operating system: memory allocation, process allocation, device input and output, etc.
libtermcap_trg	2.0.8-1 L	GPL	The libtermcap package contains a basic system library needed to access the termcap database. The termcap library supports easy access to the termcap database, so that programs can output character-based displays in a terminal-independent manner.
libtermcap_trg-devel	2.0.8-1	LGPL	This package includes the libraries and header files necessary for developing programs that will access the termcap database.

If you need to develop programs that will access the termcap database, you'll need to install this package. You'll also need to install the libtermcap package. |
mingetty_trg	0.9.4-1	GPL	The mingetty program is a lightweight, minimalist getty program for use only on virtual consoles. mingetty is not suitable for serial lines (you should use the mgetty program for that purpose).
mkboot_trg	1.0-1	LynxWorks	The mkboot utility installs a kernel on bootable media (hard disk or floppy).
mount_trg	2.9u-1	GPL	The mount package contains the mount, umount, swapon, and swapoff programs. Accessible files on your system are arranged in one big tree or hierarchy. These files can be spread out over several devices. The mount command attaches a filesystem on some device to your system's file tree. The umount command detaches a filesystem from the tree. swapon and swapoff specify and disable devices and files for paging and swapping, respectively.

Package	Version	License	Description
net-tools_trg	1.53-1	GPL	The net-tools package contains the basic tools needed for setting up networking: arp, rarp, ifconfig, netstat, ethers, and route.
netkit-base_trg	0.10-1	BSD	The netkit-base package contains the basic networking tools ping and inetd. The ping command sends a series of ICMP protocol ECHO_REQUEST packets to a specified network host and can tell you whether that machine is alive and receiving network traffic. inetd listens on certain Internet sockets for connection requests, decides which program should receive each request, and starts that program. The netkit-base package should be installed on any machine that's on a network.
pam_trg	0.68-1	GPL or BSD	PAM (Pluggable Authentication Modules) is a system-security tool that allows system administrators to set authentication policy without having to recompile programs that do authentication.
procps_trg	2.0.4-1	GPL	The procps package contains a set of system utilities that provide system information. procps includes ps, free, sessreg, skill, snice, tload, top, uptime, vmstat, w, and watch. The ps command displays a snapshot of running processes. The top command provides a repetitive update of the statuses of running processes. The free command displays the amounts of free and used memory on your system. sessreg is a simple program for managing utmp/wtmp entries for xdm sessions. The skill command sends a terminate command (or another specified signal) to a specified set of processes. The snice command is used to change the scheduling priority of specified processes. The tload command prints a graph of the

continues

Package	Version	License	Description
			current system load average to a specified TTY. The uptime command displays the current time, how long the system has been running, how many users are logged on, and system load averages for the past one, five, and fifteen minutes. The w command displays a list of the users who are currently logged on and what they're running. The watch program watches a running program. The vmstat command displays virtual memory statistics about processes, memory, paging, block I/O, traps, and CPU activity.
tcl_trg	8.0.5-1	BSD	tcl is a simple scripting language designed to be embedded into other applications. tcl is designed to be used with tk, a widget set, which is provided in the tk package. This package also includes tclsh, a simple example of a tcl application.
			If you're installing the tcl package and you want to use tcl for development, you should also install the tk and tclx packages.
util-linux_trg	2.9w-1	distributable	The util-linux package contains a large variety of low-level system utilities that are necessary for a Linux system to function. Among many features, util-linux contains the fdisk configuration tool and login program.

BlueCat Linux Pros and Cons

We now turn to our list of questions to ask any embedded Linux toolkit to see how well BlueCat Linux stacks up to the competition.

What is the size of image produced?

Like PeeWeeLinux, examined later in this chapter, BlueCat Linux suffers from the use of glibc as its C library. This makes it difficult to put a lot of functionality into an embedded device with less than 2MB of storage. However, BlueCat can fit more on the floppy disk than PeeWeeLinux, since it doesn't use syslinux to boot.

What architectures are supported?

The following target processor families are supported:

- Intel IA-32 (x86)
- PowerPC
- PowerQUICC
- ARM/ARM7/ARM9/StrongARM
- Super-H
- MIPS R3000/R4000

How easy is the toolkit to use?

The toolkit is quite straightforward and easy to use. However if you're a true believer in a graphical development environment, you'll be disappointed—it's straight text only. This works well for my style of development, but some people just don't like hacking on Makefiles.

How many optional packages are available?

I counted 381 optional packages in Appendix B of the BlueCat Linux User's Guide. Most of that stuff is completely useless for an embedded system, however (unless you consider putting the Slovenian HOWTO on your target somehow useful).

What exceptional packages are available?

The packages I reviewed were all standard Linux software. BlueCat's value-add is their build environment and toolset—they don't give you anything out of the ordinary in their target RPM packages.

How customizable is the image? How difficult is it to customize?

BlueCat Linux uses a special specification file to lay out the filesystem of the target. The specification file looks very much like a shell script, and as such, the target is completely customizable.

How much does the toolkit cost? Is a royalty involved?

In early 2001, BlueCat Linux costs anywhere from US$299 to US$20,000, depending on the support level you want to pay for.

How well is the toolkit documented? Is printed documentation available?

The documentation was up to the task of getting me started. A HOWTO would be helpful. For instance, it wasn't obvious how to add code to the target from the documentation (however, one look at the specification file was all it took).

How well is the toolkit supported? Paid support? Active list?

LynuxWorks has been around for a number of years. They have another embeddable operating system called LynxOS, so they have an established support organization. Therefore, their Linux support looks like many other software companies' support—you can buy installation support and/or incident support from them directly. As of this writing, their Web site doesn't mention any lists.

What are the requirements to use the toolkit?

The following host operating systems are supported:

- Red Hat 6.1 and 6.2
- TurboLinux Workstation, version 6.0
- Windows 98/NT/2000

Windows is supported using `cygwin`. Supporting Microsoft Windows as a hosting environment, although it may make many Linux partisans cringe, is quite a good idea. It can only serve to spread Linux to more developers.

Can a new version of the toolkit be installed without losing changes?

Even though our examples lived within the `~bluecat/bluecat` directory tree, there was no reason why they had to. You can easily upgrade BlueCat without fear of blowing away your projects.

PeeWeeLinux (*www.peeweelinux.org*)

In the words of its author, "PeeWeeLinux is an ongoing development effort to provide an environment that makes the configuration and installation of a Linux operating system on an embedded platform as easy and painless as possible."

Unlike BlueCat Linux, PeeWeeLinux is a Open Source *project*, but not a *product*. As such, it doesn't have dedicated engineering resources behind it, and probably doesn't go through a testing procedure as rigorous as that for BlueCat.

PeeWeeLinux uses `RPM` to build and maintain its packages, and has a nice text-mode build system. It specifically supports the 2.2 kernel, USB, PCMCIA, and XFree86.

Using PeeWeeLinux

I was able to install PeeWeeLinux version 0.53.23 and get my application floppy up and running in about an hour. The documentation is quite sparse, but there's enough to get you started. Generally, these are the steps I followed:

1. Download the latest distribution from one of the mirrors listed at
   `www.peeweelinux.org`. I downloaded the binary-only version, which
   was over 53MB. The version with full source is almost 200MB!

2. Untar the distribution into a filesystem with at least 150MB free (binary only).

3. Once it's untarred, you'll have a new directory called `Embedded_Build`. Change to that directory and run the `./pwlconfig` script. This script is the heart of PeeWeeLinux—a 20KB `bash` script that builds and configures your project and builds your bootable image.

4. Choose Manage Package Files and then Extract ALL binary RPM files. You won't have any packages to select until you do this.

5. PeeWeeLinux comes with a couple of example projects. I suggest you don't try to build a new project from scratch; it's difficult to tell which packages are needed for a project and which are not. Just start with one of the sample packages. For example, to start with the minimal package, just untar `examples/minimal.tgz` from the PeeWeeLinux root directory, rename `projects/minimal` to `projects/yourprojectname` and rerun `./pwlconfig`. You should then select the project using the Manage Projects menu.

   The minimal project includes all of the following:

   - Editor: `ee`
   - Kernel: basic 2.2.17 with minimal `modutils`
   - Shell: `ash`
   - System base: `bdflush`, `dev`, `filesystem`, `initscripts`, `mingetty`, `sysvinit`, `util-linux`
   - System libraries: `glibc`, `libtermcap`
   - System utilities: `fileutils`, `sh-utils`, `textutils`

6. Choose Configure Project File System to choose which packages to put in your filesystem. The minimal package almost fills up the entire floppy disk, so Minicom won't fit. However, the `microcom` package also comes with PeeWeeLinux, and it's only 12KB, so let's choose that package (under Network Serial) as an example.

7. Choose Extract File System for Project. This copies all of the contents of the packages to the `mnt` directory within your project—getting you ready for the next step.

8. Load a floppy disk into the drive and choose Load File System onto Target. If all goes well, you'll have a bootable floppy disk.

9. Boot the floppy disk. You'll have to log in—the root password is `redhat`. Once logged in, type `microcom /dev/ttySx` to run `microcom`. Change the x to `0` or `1`, depending on which serial port you're testing.

What's Included with PeeWeeLinux?

PeeWeeLinux actually comes with a lot of packages, each of which has been recompiled to fit well into an embedded Linux environment.

Package	Version	License	Description
ICAClient	3.0-1	Commercial	The Citrix Independent Computing Architecture (ICA).
XFree86	3.3.6-7	MIT	The X windows system provides the base technology for developing graphical user interfaces.
			This package contains the basic files needed for an X workstation. However, this package doesn't provide the hardware-specific X server for the video card.
XFree86-Xdpi-fonts	3.3.6-7	MIT	Where X is 75 or 100. These packages contain the fonts used on most X windows systems.
XFree86-X	3.3.6-7	MIT	Where X is any of 3DLabs, 8514, AGX, FBDev, I128, Mach32, Mach64, Mach8, Mono, P9000, S3, S3V, SVGA, VGA16, W32, or Xnest. These packages provide the hardware-specific X server for numerous video chipsets.
XFree86-libs	3.3.6-7	MIT	XFree86-libs contains the shared libraries needed by most X programs.
XFree86-stuff	3.3.6-7	MIT	Various programs and utilities built with XFree86.
XFree86-twm	3.3.6-7	MIT	A simple window manager for the X windows system.
XFree86-xdm	3.3.6-7	MIT	Manages a collection of X displays that may be on the local host or remote servers.
XFree86-xfs	3.3.6-7	MIT	Contains the font server for XFree86. xfs can also serve fonts to remote servers.
ash	0.2-2	BSD	Most Linux desktop distributions use GNU's bash (Bourne again shell). However, bash is a very large program requiring a lot of memory and storage. The ash shell is a subset of bash. It supports most bash commands, but is considerably smaller

Package	Version	License	Description
			and uses less memory. It lacks some command-line features of bash—but most embedded systems won't have users typing commands at a console anyway.
ash-static	0.2-2	BSD	The ash-static package contains a statically linked version of the ash shell. This is useful if you're not using the shared libraries.
bash	2.03-3	GPL	bash is a GNU project sh-compatible shell or command-language interpreter. bash (Bourne again shell) incorporates useful features from the Korn shell (ksh) and the C shell (csh). Most sh scripts can be run by bash without modification.
			bash offers several improvements over sh, including command-line editing, unlimited-size command history, job control, shell functions and aliases, indexed arrays of unlimited size and integer arithmetic in any base from 2 to 64. bash is ultimately intended to conform to the IEEE POSIX P1003.2/ISO 9945.2 Shell and Tools standard.
bdflush	1.5-1	None	The bdflush process starts the kernel daemon, which flushes dirty buffers back to disk (writes all unwritten data to disk). This helps to prevent the buffers from growing too stale. bdflush is normally a basic system process that must run for your system to operate properly. However, in an embedded environment you may not need it, especially if you never write back to your media.
boa	0.94.0-1	GPL	boa is a single-tasking HTTP server. That means that, unlike traditional Web servers, it doesn't fork for each incoming connection, nor does it fork many copies of itself to handle multiple connections.

continues

Package	Version	License	Description
			It internally multiplexes all of the ongoing HTTP connections, and forks only for CGI programs (which must be separate processes), automatic directory generation, and automatic file gunzipping.
busybox	0.46-2	GPL	BusyBox combines tiny versions of many common UNIX utilities into a single small executable. It provides minimalist replacements for most of the utilities you usually find in GNU fileutils, shellutils, etc.
			The utilities in BusyBox generally have fewer options than their full-featured GNU cousins; however, the options that are included provide the expected functionality and behave very much like their GNU counterparts.
			BusyBox provides a fairly complete POSIX environment for any small or embedded system.
cqcam	0.90pre11-1	GPL	A free color QuickCam (PC/parallel) control program.
dev	1.4-1	public domain	The Linux operating system uses filesystem entries to represent devices (CD-ROMs, floppy drives, etc.) attached to the machine.
			This package contains the most commonly used /dev entries required for a console-only system.
dhcp	2.0-2	distributable	A DHCP (Dynamic Host Configuration Protocol) server. Use the pump or dhcpcd package if you need a DHCP client.
dhcpcd	1.3.18pl3-1	GPL	A DHCP client.
digitemp	1.3-1	GPL	Reads temperatures from Dallas Semiconductor DS1820 digital temperature sensors.
dosfstools	2.4-1	GPL	A tool suite to create, check, and repair FAT12, FAT16, and FAT32 filesystems.

continues

Package	Version	License	Description
e2fsprogs	1.19-1	GPL	The ext2fsprogs package contains essential ext2 filesystem utilities including e2fsck, mke2fs, debugfs, dumpe2fs, tune2fs, and most of the other core ext2 filesystem utilities.
ee	1.4.2-1	GPL	An easy-to-use text editor. Intended to be usable with little or no instruction. Provides a terminal (curses based) interface. Features pop-up menus. A subset of aee.
filesystem	1.2-2	public domain	Contains the basic directory layout for the Linux operating system, including the correct permissions for the directories.
fileutils	4.0-3	GPL	The fileutils package includes a number of GNU versions of common and popular file management utilities.
fvwm2	2.2.4-4	GPL	A window manager for the X windows system. If you install fvwm2, you'll also need to install fvwm2-icons.
fvwm2-icons	2.2.4-4	GPL	The fvwm2-icons package contains icons, bitmaps, and pixmaps used by the FVWM and FVWM2 X windows system window managers.
glibc	2.1.3-6	LGPL	The glibc package contains standard libraries that are used by multiple programs on the system. In order to save disk space and memory, as well as to make upgrading easier, common system code is kept in one place and shared between programs. This particular package contains the most important sets of shared libraries: the standard C library and the standard math library. Without these two libraries, a Linux system will not function—unless you use statically linked binaries. The glibc package also contains national language (locale) support and timezone databases.

continues

Package	Version	License	Description
			The original Red Hat source RPM has been modified for PeeWeeLinux. The changes are documented in the spec file.
grep	2.4.2-1	GPL	The General Regular Expression Processor from GNU. It searches one or more files for a regular expression.
gzip	1.2.4a-1	GPL	gzip (GNU zip) is a compression utility designed to be a replacement for compress. Its main advantages over compress are much better compression and freedom from patented algorithms. The GNU Project uses it as the standard compression program for its system.
initscripts	1.5-1	public domain	The initscripts package contains the basic system scripts used to boot the system, change runlevels, and shut the system down cleanly. This package differs significantly from the Red Hat way of doing things. PeeWeeLinux supports only a single runlevel to minimize complexity.
ipchains	1.3.9-1	GPL	Linux IP firewalling chains is an update to (and hopefully an improvement upon) the Linux kernel packet-filtering code. ipchains allows you to set up firewalls and IP masquerading, etc. Install ipchains if you need to set up firewalling for your network.
ipmasqadm	0.4.2-2	distributable	This tool allows ipmasq additional setup; it's needed if you want to activate port forwarding or auto forwarding in 2.2 kernels.
iptraf	2.2.2-1	GPL	IPTraf is a console-based network-monitoring program that displays information about IP traffic. This program can be used to determine the type of traffic on your network, what kind of service is the most heavily used on what machines, among others.

Package	Version	License	Description
isapnptools	1.21b-1	GPL	The isapnptools package contains utilities for configuring ISA Plug-and-Play (PnP) cards that are in compliance with the PnP ISA Specification Version 1.0a. ISA PnP cards use registers instead of jumpers for setting the board address and interrupt assignments. The cards also contain descriptions of the resources that need to be allocated. The BIOS on your system, or isapnptools, uses a protocol described in the specification to find all of the PnP boards and allocate the resources so that none of them conflict.
			Note that the BIOS doesn't do a very good job of allocating resources. So isapnptools is suitable for all systems, whether or not they include a PnP BIOS. In fact, a PnP BIOS adds some complications. A PnP BIOS may already activate some cards so that the drivers can find them. Then these tools can unconfigure them or change their settings, causing all sorts of nasty effects. If you have PnP network cards that already work, you should read through the documentation files very carefully before you use isapnptools.
			Install isapnptools if you need utilities for configuring ISA PnP cards.
kernel-basic	2.2.14-9	GPL	This package contains a Linux kernel optimized for a generic Intel x86 CPU.
			Most popular network cards and various routing features are supported. The ext2, FAT, and iso9660 filesystems are recognized. Support for peripherals such as serial ports, parallel ports, framebuffer video, and various IDE devices are included.

continues

Package	Version	License	Description
kernel-basic	2.2.17-10	GPL	This package contains a Linux kernel in a very basic configuration.
			This kernel could be well suited for a rescue system, since most network drivers are included but most other fatty modules are disabled.
kernel-emlog	2.2.17-10	GPL	This package contains prebuilt device files for the emlog.o module.
			emlog is a Linux kernel module that makes it easy to access the most recent (and only the most recent) output from a process. It works like tail -f on a log file, except that the required storage never grows. This can be useful in embedded systems, where there isn't enough memory or disk space for keeping complete log files, but the most recent debugging messages are sometimes needed (for example, after an error is observed).
			The emlog kernel module implements a simple character-device driver. The driver acts like a named pipe that has a finite, circular buffer. The size of the buffer is easily configurable. As more data is written into the buffer, the oldest data is discarded. A process that reads from an emlog device will first read the existing buffer and then see new text as it's written.
kernel-full	2.2.17-10	GPL	This package contains a Linux kernel with most modular options enabled.
			This package is *not* a typical embedded kernel but is provided for testing purposes.
kernel-source	2.2.17-10	GPL	This package contains the kernel sources. (Perhaps providing sources in a binary package seems like a paradox. This source package is provided for the PeeWeeLinux custom kernel build process.)

Package	Version	License	Description
ldconfig	1.9.5-1	GPL	ldconfig is a basic system program that determines runtime link bindings between ld.so and shared libraries. ldconfig scans a running system and sets up the symbolic links that are used to load shared libraries properly. It also creates a cache (/etc/ld.so.cache) that speeds the loading of programs that use shared libraries.
libjpeg	6b-1	GPL	libjpeg supplies support functions for the JPEG image format, to programs that are linked to it.
libstdc++	2.9.0-1	GPL	The libstdc++ package contains a snapshot of the EGCS Standard C++ Library v3, an ongoing project to implement the ISO 14882 Standard C++ library.
libtermcap	2.0.8-4	LGPL	The libtermcap package contains a basic system library needed to access the termcap database. The termcap library supports easy access to the termcap database, so that programs can output character-based displays in a terminal-independent manner. This package has been modified for PeeWeeLinux from the original Red Hat version.
lilo	0.21-3	MIT	LILO (Linux Loader) is a basic system program that boots your Linux system. LILO loads the Linux kernel from a floppy or hard drive, boots the kernel, and passes control of the system to the kernel. LILO can also boot other operating systems.
mgetty	1.1.21-3	distributable	The mgetty package contains a "smart" getty that allows logins over a serial line (through a modem). If you're using a Class 2 or 2.0 modem, mgetty can receive faxes. If you also need to send faxes, you'll need to install the sendfax program.

continues

Package	Version	License	Description
microcom	1.01-1	GPL	microcom is a Minicom-like serial terminal emulator with scripting support. The requirement for this program was to be small enough to fit on a floppy-based Linux distribution, such as the one from the Linux Router Project. They managed to bring the executable size down under 17KB.
mingetty	0.9.4-1	GPL	The mingetty program is a lightweight, minimalist getty program for use only on virtual consoles. mingetty is not suitable for serial lines (use mgetty instead).
minicom	1.83.1-1	GPL	Minicom is a serial communications program, a UNIX clone of the well-known MS-DOS Telix program. It has ANSI color, a dialing directory, dial-a-list, script language, and so on.
modutils	2.3.9-1	GPL	This package contains the module utilities for the 2.2 kernels. Install the full package if you need to use modprobe or need to remove modules. In an embedded environment, modules generally only need to be installed. The minimal package provides insmod to install modules, and nothing else.
modutils-minimal	2.3.9-1	GPL	This package contains the module utilities for the 2.2 kernels. Install the full package if you need to use modprobe or need to remove modules. In an embedded environment, modules generally only need to be installed. The minimal package provides insmod to install modules, and nothing else.

Package	Version	License	Description
msntp	1.5-1	freely distributable	msntp can be used as an NTP client to query an NTP or SNTP server and either display the time or set the local system's time (given suitable privileges). It can be run as an interactive command, in a cron job, or as a daemon. It can be run as a daemon to provide an SNTP server for other clients.
			NTP is the Network Time Protocol (RFC 1305) and SNTP is the Simple Network Time Protocol (RFC 2030, which supersedes RFC 1769).
nano	0.9.21-1	GPL	nano (Nano's ANOther editor, or Not ANOther editor) aims to emulate Pico as closely as possible while offering a few enhancements.
			Requires ncurses.
ncftp	3.0.1-1	Artistic	ncftp is a program that implements the File Transfer Protocol. It allows a user to transfer files to and from a remote network site, and offers additional features that are not found in the standard interface.
ncurses	5.1-4	distributable	The curses library routines are a terminal-independent method of updating character screens with reasonable optimization. The ncurses (new curses) library is a freely distributable replacement for the discontinued 4.4 BSD classic curses library.
net-tools	1.54-1	GPL	The net-tools package contains the basic tools needed for setting up networking: ethers, route, and others.
netkit-base	0.16-2	BSD	The netkit-base package contains the basic networking tools ping and inetd.
			netkit-base is required on any machine running telnetd, ftpd, and other network daemons.

continues

Package	Version	License	Description
netkit-ftp	0.10-1	BSD	The `ftp` package provides the standard UNIX command-line FTP (File Transfer Protocol) client. FTP is a widely used protocol for transferring files over the Internet and for archiving files.
			If your system is on a network, you should install FTP in order to do file transfers.
netkit-telnet	0.14-3	BSD	Telnet is a popular protocol for logging into remote systems over the Internet. The `telnet` package provides a command-line Telnet client as well as a Telnet daemon, which supports remote logins into the host machine. The Telnet daemon is enabled by default. You can disable the Telnet daemon by editing `/etc/inetd.conf`.
			Install the `telnet` package if you want to Telnet to remote machines and/or support remote logins to your own machine.
netscape-navigator	4.74-2	free to use but restricted	Netscape Communicator is an all-in-one Web browser and communications suite that makes it easy to send Internet email, read newsgroups, create Web pages, and browse the World Wide Web.
			This is a reduced footprint edition without email or news client and some other "unimportant" features such as help.
networkscripts	1.1-1	public domain	The `networkscripts` package contains essential scripts and configuration files to bring up networking on the PeeWeeLinux system.
			This package is required for networking.
nullidentd	1.0-1	GPL	`nullidentd` is a minimal `identd` server. All `identd` requests are responded to with the same (false) answer. It's intended as a very small (possibly secure) daemon to run on a firewall for connections to servers that use `identd` responses.

Package	Version	License	Description
portfwd	0.15-2	GPL	portfwd, by Everton da Silva Marques, is a small C++ utility that forwards incoming TCP connections and/or UDP packets to remote hosts. It features forwarding based on originator port, multiple ports forwarded from one config file, and FTP forwarding, which requires two ports.
			Check the home page at http://nucleo.freeservers.com/portfwd for full details and features.
ppp	2.3.11-1	distributable	The ppp package contains the PPP (Point-to-Point Protocol) daemon and documentation for PPP support. The PPP protocol provides a method for transmitting datagrams over serial point-to-point links.
			The ppp package should be installed if your machine needs to support the PPP protocol.
procps	2.0.7-2	GPL	procps is a package of utilities that report on the state of the system, including the states of running processes, amount of memory available, and currently-logged-in users.
procps-ncurses	2.0.7-2	GPL	This is an add-on to procps. The binaries require ncurses to function.
pump	0.7.8-1	MIT	pump is a combined BOOTP and DHCP client daemon, which allows your machine to retrieve configuration information from a server. You should install this package if you're on a network that uses BOOTP or DHCP.
sed	3.02-1	GPL	sed, the GNU Stream Editor, copies the named files (standard input default) to the standard output, edited according to a script of commands.
setserial	2.17-1	GPL	setserial is a tool to set/report the configuration information associated with a serial port. This information includes which I/O port and which IRQ a particular serial port is using.

continues

Package	Version	License	Description
sh-utils	2.0-3	GPL	sh-utils is a package of small shell programming utilities. They're mostly compliant with POSIX.2, where applicable. The programs that can be built with this package include basename, chroot, date, dirname, echo, env, expr, factor, false, groups, hostname, id, logname, nice, nohup, pathchk, printenv, printf, pwd, seq, sleep, stty, su, tee, test, true, tty, uname, users, who, whoami, and yes.
stamp	2.0.8-1	GPL	stamp is a command-line program that processes a color or grayscale JPEG image, such as one produced by a Quickcam. It can add a graphical (and configurable) timestamp to the image. stamp can also upload the timestamped image via FTP, with the configuration of a stamprc file.
sysklogd	1.3.31-4	GPL	The sysklogd package contains two system utilities (syslogd and klogd) that provide support for system logging. syslogd and klogd run as daemons (background processes) and log system messages to sendmail logs, security logs, error logs, etc.
sysvinit	2.78-3	GPL	init is the parent of all processes. Its primary role is to create processes from a script stored in the file /etc/inittab. This package also contains well-known popular utilities such as reboot, shutdown, killall, poweroff, tellinit, sulogin, wall, etc.
tar	1.13-1	GPL	GNU tar saves many files together into a single tape or disk archive, and can restore individual files from the archive. It includes multivolume support, the ability to archive sparse files, automatic archive compression and decompression, remote archives, and special features that allow tar to be used for incremental and full

Package	Version	License	Description
			backups. It also includes rmt, the remote tape server (the mt tape-drive control program is in GNU cpio).
tcpdump	3.5.2-1	BSD	tcpdump prints out the headers of packets on a network interface. It's very useful for debugging network problems and security operations.
textutils	2.0a-1	GPL	A set of GNU utilities for modifying the contents of files, including programs for splitting, joining, comparing, and modifying files.
thttpd	2.15-1	BSD	thttpd is a simple, small, fast, and secure HTTP server. It doesn't have a lot of special features, but it suffices for most uses of the Web. It's faster than Apache and has one extremely useful feature (URL-traffic–based throttling) that no other server currently has.
tinylogin	0.78-2	GPL	TinyLogin is a suite of tiny UNIX utilities for handling logins, user authentication, changing passwords, and otherwise maintaining users and groups on an embedded system. It also provides shadow password support to enhance system security. As the name implies, TinyLogin is very small, and makes an excellent addition to an embedded system.
util-linux	2.10m-4	GPL	util-linux is a suite of essential utilities for any Linux system. Its primary audience is system integrators and DIY Linux hackers. util-linux is attempting to be portable, but the only platform it has been tested on very much is Linux i386.
vim	5.7-3	free to use but restricted	vim is an almost fully compatible version of the UNIX editor vi. Many new features have been added including multilevel undo, syntax highlighting, command-line history, online help, filename completion, and block operations.

continues

Package	Version	License	Description
			This is a minimal binary called `vi` that requires `termcap`.
`vim-ncurses`	5.7-3	free to use but restricted	This package is a minimal binary called `vim` that requires `ncurses` (see above for details on `vim`).
`vixie-cron`	3.0.1-2	distributable	The `vixie-cron` package contains the Vixie version of `cron`. `cron` is a standard UNIX daemon that runs specified programs at scheduled times. `vixie-cron` adds better security and more powerful configuration options to the standard version of `cron`.
`wget`	1.5.3-1	GPL	GNU `wget` is a freely available network utility to retrieve files from the World Wide Web using HTTP and FTP, the two most widely used Internet protocols. It works non-interactively, thus enabling users to work in the background after logging off.
`xpm`	3.4k-2	MIT	The `xpm` package contains the XPM pixmap library for the X windows system. The XPM library allows applications to display color and pixmapped images, and is used by many popular X programs.

PeeWeeLinux Pros and Cons

Let's take a look at how well PeeWeeLinux stacks up to our list of questions.

What is the size of image produced?

The image size produced by PeeWeeLinux isn't all that small. The big problem is the use of `glibc`. It can be difficult to get away from `glibc`, but for really small applications you have to do it. The `glibc` file that comes with PeeWeeLinux is just over 1MB. Using `uClibc` or even the old `libc5` may be a better choice. This does complicate the development environment somewhat, but it's worth it in terms of cost.

What architectures are supported?

PeeWeeLinux has an impressive array of x86 targets, but as of this writing, x86 only. If you're looking for PowerPC, StrongARM, etc., look elsewhere.

For x86, PeeWeeLinux supports the following environments:

- Compressed RAM disk on FAT 16 partition
- Compressed RAM disk on ext2 partition
- Uncompressed RAM disk on FAT 16 partition
- Uncompressed RAM disk on ext2 partition
- Read-only root filesystem with multiple RAM disks
- Compressed RAM disk on floppy disk without bootloader
- Compressed RAM disk on FAT 12 floppy disk with `syslinux`
- Read-write root on a single partition

How easy is the toolkit to use?

Getting started with PeeWeeLinux is fairly easy. It took less than two hours to get my first bootable floppy image running after installing the software.

How many optional packages are available?

PeeWeeLinux boasts almost 100 packages. Some of them are of dubious value within an embedded system, but most are quite useful.

What exceptional packages are available?

PeeWeeLinux gives you the tools necessary to build a Web-based configuration package, namely the `thttpd` and `boa` Web servers. However, nothing is set up for you.

There are a couple of pieces of specific hardware support that might be interesting: the Color QuickCam and the Dallas Semiconductor DS1280 digital temperature sensors.

PeeWeeLinux comes with four prebuilt Linux x86 kernels and with the kernel source in case you decide to build your own.

The authors of PeeWeeLinux have also taken the time to strip Netscape down to the minimum code required for a browser. This is helpful because the full browser suite with email and newsreader is quite large. Of course, Netscape requires X windows, and PeeWeeLinux has support for that, too.

How customizable is the image? How difficult is it to customize?

To add custom software to your project, you add the files to the Project Custom Source Path. Each file and directory within this directory is copied to the destination directory during the build process.

While this is simple and effective, it does have some drawbacks. This directory structure could quickly become polluted with cruft as you try different ideas while building your device. If you want to use part of your software in another project, it may become difficult to extract just those pieces from a big jumbled mess.

If you want to do serious development, hook into the package system of PeeWeeLinux and save the Project Custom Source Path for quick-and-dirty changes during the development process.

How much does the toolkit cost? Is a royalty involved?

PeeWeeLinux is completely free.

How well is the toolkit documented? Is printed documentation available?

Documentation for Open Source projects typically falls into two categories: "much weaker than proprietary products" and "much stronger than proprietary projects." It seems that some magic threshold must be crossed before the documentation is really there. As of this writing, the PeeWeeLinux documentation is in the former category—there's just not much there. To figure out how the product is working, you have to look at the source.

But don't let that stop you from using PeeWeeLinux if it fits well in the other categories—it's not hard to figure out how to use it.

How well is the toolkit supported? Paid support? Active list?

The PeeWeeLinux mailing list had 30–40 members as of early 2001. The package seems to be updated at least on a monthly basis. The author is available for technical support, and does short-duration consulting work.

What are the requirements to use the toolkit?

PeeWeeLinux has been tested on all versions of Red Hat Linux from 6.0 through 7.0. It is also known to work with Mandrake 7.0. You'll need 200MB of free space to install it.

Can a new version of the toolkit be installed without losing changes?

PeeWeeLinux expects your projects to be in one of its subdirectories. Because of this restriction, upgrading can be a little disconcerting—you're going to install on top of your current projects. They shouldn't be overwritten, but if they are, well, I hope you have backups.

Really, the best thing to do is remove the `projects` directory as soon as you install PeeWeeLinux and create a symbolic link to somewhere else in your filesystem.

Summary

There are a lot of variables to get under control when you're choosing an embedded Linux toolkit. Choose what's most important to you first—cost, executable size, target platform, etc.—to help pare down the list, and then start exploring.

7

The Embedded Linux Workshop

THIS CHAPTER DESCRIBES THE *EMBEDDED LINUX WORKSHOP* (*ELW*), an Open Source embedded Linux toolkit—put together specifically for this book—that makes it easy to build embedded Linux applications quickly and efficiently. As discussed in Chapter 6, "Embedded Linux Toolkits," there are already several embedded Linux toolkits available—so why would I bother to create another one? The reason is simple: I wanted to create an Open Source embedded Linux teaching aid that's well documented and simple enough to understand quickly and completely, yet powerful enough for any embedded Linux project.

Here's some basic info you need to know about using ELW:

- ELW assumes that you're using a standard PC with a BIOS to prototype your embedded application.

- ELW uses the SYSLINUX boot loader to load the kernel and root filesystem.

- ELW doesn't get into the gory details of how the processor initializes the hardware, loads the kernel and root filesystems into memory, switches the processor to 32-bit mode, and starts the kernel. These details vary wildly from processor to processor; covering them all in a single book would be impossible. The whole topic is glossed over with this simple statement: "The BIOS and SYSLINUX do that." For more information, see Chapter 4, "Booting Your Embedded Linux Device."

Of course, in your embedded Linux project, you may not have a BIOS and SYS-LINUX may not be appropriate—after all, it only works on an x86 platform. For that reason, I won't spend a lot of time on SYSLINUX, but it's a great utility that performs a specific need very well. You may even want to take a look at it when you're emulating its behavior for your own embedded design.

General Goals

These are the general goals of the Embedded Linux Workshop:

- It must be easy to learn.
- It must be useful in real-world situations.

These are the goals of the embedded Linux applications you can build with ELW:

- **Minimal code size.** The top priority of *any* embedded Linux toolkit should really be building an embedded Linux application that minimizes code size. The smaller the code, the less memory and flash required to run the application; this reduces the final assembly cost.
- **Extensibility.** The Embedded Linux Workshop strives to be as extensible as possible. Adding support for various application packages, library technologies, and processors should be conceptually easy. This is especially important in the Open Source world, where a project can take on a life of its own—if it's difficult to manage the software, that project's growth can be quite limited.
- **Upgradeability.** New versions of Open Source products can come fast and furious. If project developers want users to accept and test upgrades, they must make upgrading—and sometimes downgrading—easy. Therefore, the Embedded Linux Workshop is put together so that the embedded project you're working on doesn't live in or have much to do with a specific version of the workshop itself. You could have several versions of the workshop running on your machine at any given time, and build your project with any one of them.

I'll talk more about the goals of ELW later on in this chapter.

Of course, you may decide to use a different toolkit to build your embedded Linux product, but I hope that the concepts you learn with the Embedded Linux Workshop will be helpful in evaluating and using any other toolkit you encounter.

A Bit of History

My first "embedded" Linux application, called ShareTheNet, was not originally distributed as hardware. It's a software product that a lot of people around the world use to connect their homes and businesses to the Internet. The original idea was to enable a Windows-literate user to build a Linux-based IP masquerading router with very little effort. I got the idea after spending a week of evenings setting up IP masquerading for my home network. After spending hours getting things like DNS, DHCP, and dial-on-demand working, I realized that the typical Windows user would have little hope of getting a Linux IP masquerading box up and running. So I decided to make it easy for them and built ShareTheNet.

The design constraints for ShareTheNet were quite simple: It had to fit on a single 1.44MB floppy disk. That's it. If it wouldn't fit it on the floppy, it didn't go into the product.

This left out a lot of cool development tools. For instance, Perl, C++, and Java all have huge runtime libraries, so they were out. It also precluded some features that I'd like to have had. For instance, one of the biggest early complaints against IP masquerading was that it couldn't support H.323 connections. H.323 doesn't act like a normal TCP/IP client/server application; low-level proxies such as NAT or IP masquerading don't work well because they don't normally look at the content of the traffic—just the addressing information on the packet. Unfortunately, popular video-phone software such as Microsoft's NetMeeting relied on this protocol. Proprietary "gatekeeper" software available for Linux did a great job of allowing calls through the router. The only problem was that this software was written in C++ and was itself much bigger than a floppy disk. It just wouldn't fit. Fortunately, the problem has since been solved by a protocol-specific IP masquerading module just for H.323.

The installation process for ShareTheNet goes like this:

1. The user runs a Visual Basic program called `ShareTheNet.exe`. Its purpose is to gather user input about the specific installation and build a bootable Linux floppy disk based on that input.

2. Build the floppy disk.

3. Boot another computer with the floppy disk. The other computer would serve as the network gateway to the Internet.

The boot floppy consisted of these items:

- The Linux kernel
- A minimal `initrd.gz` file
- Optional software packages
- User-selected network drivers
- The SYSLINUX files
- A single configuration file

ShareTheNet typically boots from a floppy disk, although it can boot from a hard disk. Because the floppy is built in a Windows environment, it made much more sense for the floppy to be formatted in FAT format than in ext2. This ruled out LILO. The original version of ShareTheNet used a small `autoexec.bat` file that ran `loadlin`, but this required the floppy to have the DOS operating system on it—wasting about 1/3 of the space on the floppy. Now ShareTheNet boots from SYSLINUX, which requires very little space and is much faster than `loadlin`. SYSLINUX requires two files on the floppy disk: `syslinux.cfg` (the SYSLINUX configuration file), and `ldlinux.sys` (a 5KB file that contains the code that loads the Linux kernel and `initrd.gz` files into memory and runs the kernel).

The following procedure is the ShareTheNet boot sequence:

1. The Linux kernel decompresses itself and the `initrd.gz` file and starts running. The uncompressed `initrd.gz` image becomes the root RAM disk.

2. After the kernel readies itself and loads all the built-in device drivers, it runs the `/linuxrc` script from within the `initrd.gz` RAM disk.

3. The `/linuxrc` script loads and uncompresses other packages from the boot media. These packages are stored as a compressed tar.

4. The `ldconfig` command runs to rebuild the shared library cache (`/etc/ld.so.cache`). This is done because some of the optional packages require a shared library or two that are not normally needed. The `ldconfig` command must run so those shared libraries can be found by the loader.

5. Package-specific startup scripts run next. This is how most of the services start, such as `identd`, `named`, `dhcpd` (server), and `dhcpcd` (client).

   As shown in Chapter 3, "Software Configuration," each script is responsible for taking parameters out of the `/mnt/envi` file and building any and all configuration files necessary. Usually this can be done with a few shell-script commands, but sometimes a whole C program must be written to build the configurations. This is the case for `named`—its configuration files are complicated enough that a shell script was too difficult to write.

6. The startup script is built and executed. ShareTheNet users are able to administer the software by using a Web-based configuration program. However, some things are just not configurable enough, so users can also add their own startup commands by using the browser. These commands can do anything, but are usually used to enable traffic back into the local network that would be blocked (such as ICQ traffic). These commands execute at the final phase of the ShareTheNet boot process.

Requirements

The years I've spent making ShareTheNet work have taught me many lessons in how to make Linux perform in a very limited environment. After looking at the many "embedded Linux" products available for free or fee today, I felt that a simple, well explained, nuts-and-bolts example of an extremely small Linux toolkit would serve the developer community well. Therefore, I decided to risk even more hours of staring blankly at messages like the following while building the Embedded Linux Workshop:

```
Kernel panic: No init found. Try passing init= option to kernel.
```

The workshop doesn't try to be all things to all people. As I mentioned earlier, I put it together primarily as a teaching aid, but I've been using it as the basis of all of my embedded Linux projects. Let's look in a bit more detail at the requirements for the Embedded Linux Workshop:

- It must run on a very common hardware platform, so anyone can use it.

- It must be small enough so that someone trying to learn about embedded Linux software systems can understand it completely, with only a few days' work.

- The product of the Embedded Linux Workshop is a single 1.44MB floppy disk that can be used to boot a machine into the embedded application. This is almost certainly not what your final product will actually *do*, but it gives you a reasonable goal, allowing you to use hardware that's easily available. If you were to use flash in this project, you probably would have to buy extra hardware before getting started.

- It must be very well documented so that none of the pieces are mysterious. None of the binaries should be scraped from someone else's package, unless complete source is available.

- The build environment must not have "hidden steps." That is, every piece of software that ends up on the floppy must be built from source using instructions that are available as part of the toolkit itself.

- Every piece of the toolkit must be available under Open Source license.

- The sample applications should be very simple, so they don't detract from the main point—the code that gets the computer from power-off to running application.

Hardware

- **Development platform.** The obvious hardware platform for the Embedded Linux Workshop is the ubiquitous PC. A complete development platform capable of hosting the Embedded Linux Workshop can be purchased for little more than the cost of a good garden hose. You'll want to make sure that this computer has at least one free serial port and is networkable.

- **Workbench computer.** Someone is probably willing to give you the old 486 that you'll need as your workbench computer. They may even be willing to pay you to haul it away! It should have at least 8MB of memory to be useful.

- **Professional choice.** If you're developing software for a living, bigger is better. Buy a system with a large hard drive, lots of memory, and a large, crisp display. The display is especially important, since you'll probably have a lot of windows open all at once. I personally like to do as much as possible on my laptop computer. That way, I can work on my projects from anywhere.

Software

- **Linux distribution.** Choose your favorite Linux distribution. I personally like Red Hat, but any choice should be fine.

- **Professional choice.** If you're developing software for a living, it pays to have the best equipment possible. The most valuable asset of professional developers is *time*, and saving time is usually worth the cost. When analyzing what steps a developer actually goes through during the development process, you'll usually find that a large block of time is spent in the debugging cycle during active development. (See the next section for more on the debugging cycle.)

Debugging Your Application

When applied to an embedded Linux application, the term *debugging cycle* refers to the steps necessary to build the software, move it to the workbench machine, boot the workbench machine under the new version, and get the running software to the point where you're currently developing or debugging. The shorter the debugging cycle, the faster you can develop. In a typical environment, you may end up running through the debugging cycle several dozen times in a given day, so it's wise to spend some time and money shortening the debugging cycle.

Sometimes debugging cycles can be really short; the best case is when you're using an interpreted language. You save the code and run the application right away. Other times you may have to do some time-consuming task such as burn the code into a PROM before the debugging cycle is complete.

When developing any embedded application, the most time-consuming activity usually is waiting while the computer creates the boot media, and then waiting again for that media to load on the workbench computer. I've found that the best way to shorten this debugging cycle is to use a product such as VMware and run the software on a virtual machine within the development machine. That's exactly what I did to develop the sample applications for this book. Before using VMware, I had to create floppy disk images and then use the Linux dd command to dump the images out to a floppy drive. After that was done, I would take the floppy out of the development machine and boot the workbench computer from it. The entire cycle took about five minutes, from the time I was done editing source to the time I was running the application, limiting me to about 12 rebuilds an hour. Using VMware, I don't have to move any media from place to place; the build script takes care of moving the image to the proper place for VMware. I just run the build script and then power up the VMware machine when the image is ready. The whole process takes just under $1^1/2$ minutes, allowing me to do more than 40 rebuilds per hour.

Of course, you don't just rebuild over and over again, but there are distinct advantages to having a quick debugging cycle:

- Higher productivity
- Better retention of the programmer's "working set" of knowledge about a problem

The other advantage to using VMware is that you don't actually have to get access to more hardware to build another machine. And since the virtual machines can be networked together and to the outside world, they can act very much like the real machine you're building.

Of course, the VMware machines won't have access to specialized hardware in your production machine, so they can't usually be used for the entire development process. But if you start by using this technique and move away from it only when you have to start integrating with the real hardware, you can save a lot of time to market.

Installing the Embedded Linux Workshop

Installing the Embedded Linux Workshop is generally quite painless. There are basically two different methods: CVS and FTP. Using the CVS method, you can download the most cutting-edge version of the software. This can be a little dangerous; you may end up breaking your development environment if another developer uploads some broken code. Therefore, most people like the alternative method: Download an FTP archive of a known good version of the code. That's the method described in the following steps. (If you want to use CVS, see the ELW Web site at `http://elw.sourceforge.net`.)

1. Acquire root privileges for your machine if you don't already have them. Because the Embedded Linux Workshop mounts and unmounts filesystems, there's really no way to run it except as root.

2. Download the Embedded Linux Workshop. It's available from `http://elw.sourceforge.net` or `ftp://elw.sourceforge.net/pub/elw/`. There are a lot of files to download if you want the full source to the ELW. However, for now you only need the workshop itself. It will be named `elw-X.Y.Z.tgz`, where `X.Y.Z` is the current version number. If you want to just experiment with the Embedded Linux Workshop, you won't need to download all of the source code to all of the packages. However, if you're targeting a non–x86 CPU or want to do more than fool around with the software, you'll have to download most of the source code over time.

3. Change to the `/usr/local` directory:

   ```
   cd /usr/local
   ```

   This is the easiest place to install the Embedded Linux Workshop. If you decide to install it somewhere else, be sure to point your `/usr/local/elw` symbolic link to the right place.

4. Install the Embedded Linux Workshop in the /usr/local directory:

    ```
    tar xvzf /tmp/elw-X.Y.Z.tgz
    ```

    The command above assumes that you downloaded the elw-X.Y.Z.tgz tarball into the /tmp directory.

5. Remove the old elw symbolic link and create a new one that points to the directory you just installed:

    ```
    rm -f elw && ln -s elw-X.Y.Z elw
    ```

    If you need to revert to a previous version of the Embedded Linux Workshop, you can just point this symlink back to the old version.

6. Remove any old /usr/bin/elw links and create a new one that points to the elw script in the elw package:

    ```
    (cd /usr/bin && rm -f elw && ln -s /usr/local/elw/bin/elw elw)
    ```

Your First Embedded Linux Workshop Project

If you read this book straight through, by the time you're done with it you'll be quite tired of the Minicom program. I use it in several examples. The great thing about Minicom is that it doesn't require the test bed machine to have any more hardware than a regular off-the-shelf PC—it just needs a serial port. And it actually does something useful!

The preceding section walked you through the installation of the Embedded Linux Workshop. In this section, I'll give you a step-by-step procedure to build a bootable floppy disk that will directly run Minicom.

1. Change to the directory where you want your new project to live:

    ```
    cd ~yourhome/projects
    ```

2. Use the elw command installed earlier to create the new project. Several directories and files are created within the new minicom directory.

    ```
    elw --newproject minicom
    ```

3. Change to the src directory:

    ```
    cd minicom/arch/i386/src
    ```

4. Create a minicom subdirectory to store the source for Minicom:

    ```
    mkdir minicom
    ```

5. Change to the new minicom directory.

    ```
    cd minicom
    ```

6. Download Minicom from http://www.pp.clinet.fi/~walker/minicom.html. If it's not there, try http://www.freshmeat.net to find it. If you have trouble downloading it, use http://ftpsearch.lycos.com to search for the filename, and then choose a site near you from which to download. At the time of this writing, the latest version was 1.83.1.

7. Untar `minicom` (if you want to see the files that are created, change `xzf` in the command to `xvzf`):

   ```
   tar xzf minicom-1.83.1.src.tar.gz
   ```

8. Create a symbolic link named `minicom` that points to the file `minicom-1.83.1`:

   ```
   ln -s minicom-1.83.1 minicom
   ```

   This symbolic link will be used in the `opt/minicom/Makefile`. If you decide to upgrade to a later version of Minicom, you can just change the symbolic link to point to the new version.

9. Change to the `minicom` source directory:

   ```
   cd minicom/src
   ```

   We have to make a small change to the Minicom source code to make sure that it works properly in our mini-environment. We'll do this by removing a Minicom security feature that's unnecessary in our embedded application.

10. In `minicom.c`, search for the following line:

    ```
    if (real_uid == 0 && dosetup == 0) {
    ```

    Now delete about 61 lines—up to, but not including the following line:

    ```
    buf[0] = 0;
    ```

    If these lines are not removed, Minicom will bail out at this point. Since we don't have to be concerned with permissions and correct users in our embedded environment, it's safe to just skip this code.

    Save your changes.

11. Make the `minicom` executable file:

    ```
    make
    ```

12. Change to the kernel source directory:

    ```
    cd ../../../kernel
    ```

13. Download the current production Linux kernel from `ftp://ftp.kernel.org/pub/linux/kernel`. At the time of this writing, the latest version was 2.2.15.

    It shouldn't really matter which version of the kernel you use for this exercise. Anything from version 2.0 through 2.4+ should work just fine. However, the binary-only DiskOnChip driver may have trouble with some kernels. It's best to use the kernel on which the DiskOnChip driver is compiled. That may be difficult to do until you try it with one kernel and it complains.

14. Untar the kernel:

    ```
    tar xzf linux-2.2.15.tar.gz
    ```

    When you're done, there will be a new directory named `linux`. Normally, as soon as I untar a kernel I rename it to `linux-x.y.z` and create a symbolic link named `linux` back to it, so I'll know what this file is later on. Be very careful not to blow away your current sources if you already have a `linux` directory.

15. Change to the kernel directory:

    ```
    cd linux
    ```

16. Configure the kernel using the `make menuconfig` command:

    ```
    make menuconfig
    ```

    The following options are based on a 2.2.15 Intel kernel—your kernel configuration may differ. Turn on these options with an asterisk (not an *M*); everything else should be turned off to save space. You'll have to go into each of the top-level menus, even those not listed here, to make sure that they're off.

    Processor Type and features

    386 processor family

    1G Maximum Physical Memory

    Loadable module support

    Enable loadable module support

    General Setup

    Kernel support for ELF binaries

    Block Devices

    Normal PC floppy disk support

    RAM disk support

    Initial RAM disk (initrd) support

    Character devices

    Virtual Terminal

    Support for console on virtual terminal

    Standard/generic (dumb) serial support

    Filesystems

    DOS FAT fs support

    MSDOS fs support

    VFAT (Windows-95) fs support

    /proc filesystem support

    Second extended fs support

    Console Drivers

    VGA text console

17. Build the kernel dependencies and then the kernel itself. We don't need to make any modules for this kernel, but if we did, we would add the word `modules` to the command line (make dep bzImage modules):

    ```
    make dep bzImage
    ```

18. Change back to the root directory of your project:

    ```
    cd ~yourname/projects/minicom
    ```

19. Create the Minicom package directories:

    ```
    mkdir -p opt/minicom/bin opt/minicom/etc/rc
    ```

20. In the Embedded Linux Workshop, each `opt` package can have a Makefile. The Makefile has three targets: `everytime`, `binaries`, and `dependencies`. The `everytime` target is normally not used. The `binaries` target is used to rebuild any binaries whose source has changed since the last build and then move those binaries into the `opt` package. Once in the package, the binaries are then stripped. Finally, the `dependencies` target lists any dependencies for the `opt` package. For instance, the `minicom` executable depends on the `ncurses` library. Obviously, you don't have to use the `cat` command to build the Makefile: it's just the most convenient method. Here's the set of commands; note that the indented lines are indented with a single tab:

    ```
    cat > opt/minicom/Makefile

    everytime:

    binaries:
        @(cd ../../src/minicom/minicom/src &amp;&amp; make)
        @cp -f ../../src/minicom/minicom/src/minicom bin
        @strip bin/minicom
        @strip --remove-section=.note --remove-section=.comment bin/minicom

    dependencies:
        @echo "libncurses"
    ```

    Press Ctrl+D here.

21. The Embedded Linux Workshop comes complete with a set of startup scripts that work similarly to the Red Hat startup scripts. Each script in the `/etc/rc` directory that begins with the letter *S* is executed in increasing sort order. Naming a script `S99{something}` implies that it should be the last script to run and that it may not return to the caller. Here's the set of commands:

    ```
    cat > opt/minicom/etc/rc/S99minicom

    #!/bin/sh
    echo "Press a key for minicom..."
    read x
    minicom -s
    ```

    Press Ctrl+D here.

    We use the `-s` option so Minicom will go directly into setup mode. It defaults to `COM2`; change that setting if necessary.

    In a real device, you would create a `minicom` configuration file and let it start directly. You also wouldn't force the user to press a key to start, but this way you can see any bootup error messages before Minicom erases them.

22. Now make the script executable:

    ```
    chmod a+x opt/minicom/etc/rc/S99minicom
    ```

23. Create the `terminfo` for the console. This file contains the definitions of escape sequences for the console for operations such as clearing the screen and drawing lines:

    ```
    cp -P /usr/share/terminfo/l/linux opt/minicom
    ```

24. Run the `elw` command:

    ```
    elw
    ```

25. Choose the Build Binaries option to build the binaries. Unless you take the time to download all the source files for the Embedded Linux Workshop, most of the binaries will fail to build. That's okay; the binaries that ship will work. You must rerun this option each time you make a change.

26. Choose the Build Image option to build the Linux files and image.

27. Insert a blank, formatted floppy into your $3^1/2$-inch drive and choose the Build Floppy option to build the bootable floppy.

28. When the build is complete, move the floppy from your build machine to the test machine and boot it. If all goes well, you'll get the following message:

    ```
    Press a key for minicom...
    ```

29. Pressing a key should start the Minicom program. If you connect a serial modem to your serial port, you should be able to dial out. You may get a couple of errors during the boot process—one about the /etc/fstab file missing, and another about /etc/rc/P* missing. You can safely ignore them.

A Tour of the Embedded Linux Workshop

As the preceding section shows, using the Embedded Linux Workshop is fairly straightforward. The way in which the toolkit was put together was also straightforward. When designing the toolkit, emphasis was placed on simplicity and expandability.

The Embedded Linux Workshop Directories

A project using the Embedded Linux Workshop uses two unconnected directory trees: one for the specific project and one for the Embedded Linux Workshop itself. This section deals with the Embedded Linux Workshop directories and files. The next section deals with the project files.

The Top-Level Directory

The top-level directory contains a very few files and a few directories. This makes the directory easy to understand and expand on. The files in the top-level directory are described in the following table.

File	Description
CHANGES	A free-format change log.
COPYING	A copy of the GNU Public License. The ELW package is covered under the GPL. However, it's important to remember that the software you build with the ELW need not be covered under the GPL. You can use the ELW to compile software and produce images that are not themselves covered under the GPL. Your project contains a config file that can name other directories to search for binaries to load onto the image you're creating. Again, these binaries don't have to be covered under the GPL.
VERSION	The current version of the Embedded Linux Workshop. This is not the version of the product you create; it's the version number of the tool you used to create the image.

These are the directories in the root of the Embedded Linux Workshop:

Directory	Contents
arch	One subdirectory for each of the architectures supported.
bin	elw Perl script. This script displays the elw menu and runs through the build process. It also contains all of the style scripts. The style scripts know how to build one or more image styles.
doc	Documentation for the current release of the Embedded Linux Workshop.
opt	Architecture-neutral files for each of the optional packages that the Embedded Linux Workshop supports.
tools	Tool chains for the various architectures that the Embedded Linux Workshop supports.

arch//src*

The arch/*/src directory contains dozens of subdirectories, one for each source module that the Embedded Linux Workshop supports for a given architecture. Each architecture may support a different set of applications requiring a different set of source modules. Within each source module directory is at least one source archive, an extracted archive in a subdirectory, and a symbolic link pointing to that extracted archive. For example, within the arch/i386/src/sed directory are the following entries:

File	Description
sed-3.02.tar.gz	The original source code for sed. It's important to keep this file because you may need it to find out what you changed to make your specific version work. This is especially important if you have to change the Makefile to support your architecture. Just be sure not to blow away your changes if you re-extract the file in the current directory.

continues

File	Description
sed-3.02	The extracted source. Any changes you need to make for your environment go here.
sed	A symbolic link to sed-3.02. All references to anything in the directory should be made through this symbolic link. That way, if you upgrade to sed version 4.0 some time in the future, you can simply download the source code into the arch/i386/src/sed directory, extract it to sed-4.0, make your changes, and point the sed symbolic link to the new directory. None of the build scripts or anything else needs to know about the change.
README	It's nice to know something about the packages in the directories, where they came from, what they're used for, etc. This file is for the ELW developer's use.

arch/*/opt

The arch/*/opt directory contains the *compiled object* produced by the build process. Everything in this directory is normally rebuilt every time you select build from the elw menu. However, if the build process for an opt fails, the directory is left intact; this way, the ELW can be distributed without all of the source. We don't do this because we're trying to hide the source; we do this because the source is really big—hundreds of megabytes. It's far better to just download the source you're actually interested in.

bin/elw

The heart of the Embedded Linux Workshop is the elw Perl script. Your author is not a Perl monk—indeed, he barely knows where the Church of Perl is—so the elw script looks a lot more like C code than line noise. Hopefully, it's readable for you.

Usage

Typing elw --help at the command line produces the following:

```
Usage:
elw [Options]
Options:
 --config DIR        Tell elw where project dir is.
 --define NAME       Define NAME. Can be used as flag in config.
 --execute CMD       Execute a CMD other than menu. See source.
 -?, --help          Show this usage message.
 -m DIR,--elwhome DIR Set ELWHOME if it's not /usr/local/elw
                     or already set in $ELWHOME env variable.
 --newproject DIR    Create a new project in DIR.

 -v, --verbose       Be verbose.
```

The Code

Let's take a look at the code. In the interest of space, much of the code is left out—just the interesting bits are reproduced here. To look at the rest of the code, you'll have to download the Embedded Linux Workshop.

```perl
#!/usr/bin/perl
####################################################################
# elw: Build an Embedded Linux Workshop project
# This code is distributed under the terms and conditions of the
# General Public License (GPL)
####################################################################
use Getopt::Long;


####################################################################
# Parse command line
####################################################################
$VERB=`basename $0`; chomp $VERB;
$ELWHOME="";
$CONFIG="";
$EXECUTE="";
%DEFINES = ();
GetOptions(
        "elwhome|m=s"    =>     \$ELWHOME,
        "config=s"       =>     \$CONFIG,
        "define=s"       =>     \%DEFINES,
        "execute=s"      =>     \$EXECUTE,
        "help|?"         =>     \$HELP,
        "newproject=s"   =>     \$NEWPROJECTNAME,
        "verbose|v"      =>     \$VERBOSE,
);
$ELWHOME=$ENV{"ELWHOME"}      if ($ELWHOME eq '');
$ELWHOME="/usr/local/elw"     if ($ELWHOME eq '');
chomp($CONFIG=`pwd`)          if ($CONFIG eq '');
$EXECUTE="menu_run"           if ($EXECUTE eq '');
usage()                       if ($HELP);
```

One thing I really like about Perl is the do_this() if (this_is_true); construction. It makes the code much more readable—whenever I write C code, I find myself missing it.

```perl
####################################################################
# Calculated constants
####################################################################
$ELW_VERSION    = qx(cat $ELWHOME/VERSION 2>dev/null);
chomp($ELW_VERSION);
if ($ELW_VERSION eq ""){
        print "$0: Set the ELWHOME environment variable.\n";
        exit;
}
```

This finds the ELW version and verifies that the $ELWHOME variable points to the Embedded Linux Workshop's home directory.

```
if (      ("$CONFIG" eq "")  ||
          ("$CONFIG" eq "/") ||
          (! -d "$CONFIG")    ||
          (! -f "$CONFIG/config")
   ){
          die "$0: '$CONFIG' is not a valid config directory\n"
   }
```

This verifies that the $CONFIG variable is pointed to a good project. I'll talk more about projects in a later section.

```
@OPTDIR=("$CONFIG","$ELWHOME");            # OPTDIR - where to look for opts
```

The @OPTDIR variable tracks the possible locations of opt packages. The config and *.style files can also add to this variable if they need to define other places where opt directories may be found. Not that the $CONFIG directory (where the specific project we're working on lives) is named first. This way, you can modify an opt package for a specific project.

```
#####################################################################
# Load in configuration file
#####################################################################
eval `cat $CONFIG/config`;

if ( ! -r "$ELWHOME/bin/$STYLE.style" ){
        die "Unable to load style: $ELWHOME/bin/$STYLE.style";
}
eval `cat $ELWHOME/bin/$STYLE.style`;
```

Ah, the power (and peril) of self-modifying Perl code. The first eval loads the configuration file for the project. Yes, the configuration file is simply Perl source code—so it can do anything. Not only can you add simple *name=value* pairs (such as doing the necessary task of setting the $STYLE variable to name the build style of your choice), but you could do such things as add options to the menu, and so on.

The second eval loads the style chosen by the $CONFIG file.

```
#####################################################################
# main()...
#####################################################################
eval $EXECUTE;
```

Most likely, the $EXECUTE variable contains menu_run, so it will run the menu. But you can run specific commands by using the -e option as the usage explains.

bin/syslinux.style

The syslinux.style script fragment is loaded into the running elw script when the $STYLE variable is set to syslinux in the project's config file. When you create a new project using the elw --newproject command, this is the default project selected in the configuration file. `syslinux.style`, like all `.style` files, contains the code to actually build the target image. It takes as input the `arch/*/opt` directories, the kernel binary, and any startup code, and outputs files into the `obj` directory within the project.

Briefly, the `syslinux.style` file looks like this:

```
####################################################################
# syslinux.style:      ELW .style perl scriptlet to build a syslinux
#                      image
# This code is distributed under the terms and conditions of the
# General Public License (GPL)
####################################################################


####################################################################
# Simple constants
####################################################################
$REQUIRED_DEV   = "console fd0 hda1 null zero";
$REQUIRED_DEV   = "$REQUIRED_DEV vcs0 vcs1 vcs2 vcs3 vcs4";
$REQUIRED_DEV   = "$REQUIRED_DEV vcs5 vcs6 vcs7 vcs8 vcs9";
$REQUIRED_DEV   = "$REQUIRED_DEV tty0 tty1 tty2 tty3 tty4";
$REQUIRED_DEV   = "$REQUIRED_DEV tty5 tty6 tty7 tty8 tty9";
$REQUIRED_DEV   = "$REQUIRED_DEV " . `basename $APP_ROOT`;
```

Only a very few devices are absolutely *required* to boot. Most of these are just nice to have floating around in the image. `/dev` files cost very little in the image, so don't be afraid to add them.

```
####################################################################
# Update items from the config file
# add later items to top of list
####################################################################
@OPT=("syslinux",@OPT);
@OPT=("busybox",@OPT);
@OPT=("libc",@OPT);
@OPT=("halt",@OPT);
@OPT=("insmod",@OPT);
@OPT=("expr",@OPT);
@OPT=("ash",@OPT);
@OPT=("base",@OPT);
```

The `@OPT` array lists the `opt` packages that are part of a project. These `opt` packages are required for every project of this style. It doesn't matter whether the package is accidentally named twice in the array; duplicates are culled. The Makefile in each `opt` package names the packages on which that `opt` package depends, so some packages that are not specifically named anywhere may also make it into the project.

```
####################################################################
# image
####################################################################
sub image {
```

The `image()` function actually takes all the bits and pieces lying around in the
`arch/*/opt` directories and puts them all together, along with the kernel, into a
bootable image.

```
# Some locals
# ----------
my($BUILD)="$CONFIG/.build";
my($MNT)="$BUILD/mnt";
my($TMP)="$BUILD/tmp";
my($IMG)="$CONFIG/obj/rootfs";
my($IMAGEROOT)="$CONFIG/obj/imageroot";
my($DISK)="$CONFIG/obj/image";
my($CFG)="$TMP/CONFIG";
my($REPORT) = "\n----------------------------------------------------------\n";

# Setup
# -----
sy("umount $MNT 2> /dev/null");
if (esy("(cd $CONFIG && rm -rf $BUILD)")){return;}
if (esy("mkdir -p $MNT")){return;}
if (esy("mkdir -p $TMP")){return;}
if (esy("rm -rf $IMG.gz $IMG $DISK")){return;}
```

After creating some local shortcut variables, it sets up by making sure that nothing is
left over from the last build, and creating the local `$TMP` directory for building and the
`$MNT` for the new root filesystem.

```
# Update the build number
# -----------------------
my($APP_BILD)=`cat $CONFIG/BUILD 2> /dev/null`;
$APP_BILD = $APP_BILD + 1;
if (esy("echo $APP_BILD > $CONFIG/BUILD")) {return;}
```

Each build is numbered, so you can easily tell if you have two different versions of
code.

```
# Create the image file, put a filesystem on it and mount it
# ----------------------------------------------------------
if (esy("dd if=/dev/zero of=$IMG bs=512 count=$INITRDSZ")) {return;}
if (esy("/sbin/mkfs.ext2 -O none -F -vm0 -N $INITRDINODES $IMG")) {return;}
if (esy("mount -t ext2 -o loop $IMG $MNT")) {return;}
```

This is where it starts to get interesting. A brand new file of all zeros is created to store
the root filesystem. It's important to start out with a fresh file every time, since empty
parts of the filesystem will compress better if they're all zeros than if they contain
garbage left over from a previous build.

Once the new image is created with the dd command, a filesystem is created on top of it with the mkfs.ext2 command. Finally, the empty filesystem is mounted.

```
# Tell application about itself
# ----------------------------
my($now) = `date +%Y%m%d`; chomp($now);
sy("echo export APP_DATE=\\\"$now\\\" >> $CFG");
sy("echo export APP_ROOT=\\\"$APP_ROOT\\\" >> $CFG") if ($APP_ROOT ne "");
sy("echo export APP_NAME=\\\"$APP_NAME\\\" >> $CFG") if ($APP_NAME ne "");
sy("echo export APP_SNAM=\\\"$APP_SNAM\\\" >> $CFG") if ($APP_SNAM ne "");
if ($APP_VERS ne ""){
    @VERS=split( /\./, $APP_VERS );
    sy("echo export APP_VERS=\\\"$APP_VERS\\\" >> $CFG");
    sy("echo export APP_VMAJ=\\\"$VERS[0]\\\" >> $CFG");
    sy("echo export APP_VMIN=\\\"$VERS[1]\\\" >> $CFG");
    sy("echo export APP_VREL=\\\"$VERS[2]\\\" >> $CFG");
}
sy("echo export APP_BILD=\\\"$APP_BILD\\\" >> $CFG") if ($APP_BILD ne "");
sy("echo export APP_UPGR=\\\"$APP_UPGR\\\" >> $CFG") if ($APP_UPGR ne "");


# Copy the CONFIG file to the obj directory
# -----------------------------------------
sy("cp -f $CFG $CONFIG/obj");
```

The CONFIG file appears in the root directory of the application's root filesystem. It contains static information about the application: its name, version number, build date, and so on.

```
# Include optional packages in rootfs.gz
# --------------------------------------
for my $pkgflg (@OPT){
    my ($pkg,$flg) = optparse( $pkgflg );
    print "-----------------------------------------------------------\n";
    print "                               $pkg\n";
    print "-----------------------------------------------------------\n";
    $OPTDSTDIR = optmake( $pkg, 0 );

        # Remove files then add them from this directory
        if ( 1+index( $flg,"m")){
           if (esy("cd $OPTDSTDIR/; tar czf $CONFIG/obj/$pkg.tgz *")){return};
        } else {
           if (esy(
           "cd $OPTDSTDIR && RM=`find . -type f -print` && cd $TMP && rm -f \$RM"
             )){return;}
           if (esy("(cd $OPTDSTDIR/; tar cf - *) | (cd $TMP; tar xf -)")){return};
    }
}
print "===========================================================\n";
```

Essentially, this code copies all of the files in each of the opt packages that this project uses into a directory that will become the root filesystem. We have to delete all the filenames in the destination directory before we copy because symbolic links that are already there will cause trouble.

```
# Copy requred devices and user specified devices
# ------------------------------------------------
if (esy("(cd /dev;tar cf - $REQUIRED_DEV)¦(cd $TMP/dev;tar xf -)")){return;}
sy("[ -n \"$DEV\" ] && (cd /dev;tar cf - $DEV)¦(cd $TMP/dev;tar xf -)");
```

As noted earlier, some devices are required by the style. Others (the ones named in the $DEV variable) are enumerated in the project's config file. Note that we cheat a little and just grab the device files from the host machine's /dev directory. This could pose a problem if the Linux version on your target differs greatly from that on your host machine. Be careful!

```
# Configure the shared libraries
# ------------------------------
if (!$STYLE_UCLIBC){
        return if (esy("cp $ELWHOME/arch/$TARGET_ARCH/opt/libc/nomedia/ldconfig
            ➥$TMP/bin/temp"));
        return if (esy("/usr/sbin/chroot $TMP /bin/temp -v"));
        return if (esy("rm -f $TMP/bin/temp"));
}
```

The syslinux.style is set up for dynamic libraries. As such, the copied opt directories should contain all the libraries necessary for all the application binaries to run. Once those libraries are copied, we must run the ldconfig command to set up the dynamic library cache properly.

```
# Fix ownership
# -------------
if (esy("cd $TMP && chown -R root:root *")) {return;}
```

syslinux.style assumes that UNIX security is of no concern, which is almost certainly true in an embedded application.

```
# Copy tmp to the new filesystem
# ------------------------------
if (esy("(cd $TMP; tar cf - *) ¦ (cd $MNT; tar xf -)")) {return;}
$REPORT = $REPORT . `df -h $MNT` . "\n";
if (esy("umount $MNT")) {return;}
$REPORT = $REPORT . `ls -l $IMG` ;
if (esy("gzip -9 $IMG")) {return;}
$REPORT = $REPORT . `ls -l $IMG.gz` ;
```

Until now, we haven't actually done anything to the filesystem we created at the beginning of this script. Everything has been done in a directory on the host machine (in the directory named in the $TMP variable). This set of code copies the directory tree we've been building to the filesystem we created and then unmounts it. This way we get the maximum possible compression.

```
# Cleanup
# -------
if (esy("rm -rf $TMP")){return;}

# Create the obj/imageroot & copy files to it
# --------------------------------------------
return if (esy("cd $CONFIG/obj && rm -rf imageroot && mkdir imageroot"));
return if (esy("cp $LINUX/$KERNEL $IMAGEROOT"));
return if (esy("cp $IMG.gz $IMAGEROOT"));
return if (esy("cp $ELWHOME/arch/$TARGET_ARCH/opt/syslinux/nomedia/ldlinux.sys
              ➡$IMAGEROOT"));
foreach $file (`(cd $CONFIG/mnt && ls )`){
        chomp $file;
        return if (esy("cp $CONFIG/mnt/$file $IMAGEROOT"));
}
```

We now gather all the pieces that don't go into the root filesystem (the kernel, pieces of SYSLINUX, and so on) into a directory that will become the floppy image.

```
# Create blank, make the filesystem, mount it & copy files to it
# --------------------------------------------------------------
return if (esy("/sbin/mkfs.msdos -f 1 -C $DISK $DISK_BLOCKS"));
return if (esy("mount -t msdos -o loop $DISK $MNT"));
foreach $file (`(cd $IMAGEROOT && ls )`){
        chomp $file;
        return if (esy("cp $IMAGEROOT/$file $MNT"));
}
$REPORT = $REPORT . `df -h $MNT` . "\n";
```

We then create a floppy image and copy all the files we just gathered onto the mounted floppy image.

```
# Unmount the image
# -----------------
return if (esy("umount $MNT"));

# Syslinux the image
# ------------------
return if (esy("cd $CONFIG && rm -rf $BUILD"));
return if (esy("($ELWHOME/arch/$TARGET_ARCH/opt/syslinux/nomedia/syslinux
          ➡$DISK )"));

print $REPORT;
}
```

Finally, we unmount the image and run SYSLINUX on it so it can boot.

opt/

Each directory within the opt tree contains the Makefile for that optional package, any directories that are named by the Makefile (unless the Makefile creates them itself), and any miscellaneous files that are specific to the package but are not created elsewhere.

opt//Makefile*

The Makefile within the root of each opt directory has one or more of these targets:

Directory	Description
binaries	This target attempts to make the binaries in each of the source directories by changing to the root of the source directory and running make. The binaries target then copies the pieces it wants from the source directory structure to one of its own directories. It then strips it if necessary, attempting to make each binary as small as possible.
	This target is used by the elw Perl script when the user selects Build Binaries from the menu. Before the script runs the make binaries command, the entire opt directory is copied to the arch/*/opt directory. *Binary executable files will never appear in the opt directory, only in the arch/*/opt directory*.
slowbinaries	This target works just like the binaries target, but is intended for packages that take a long time to build, such as the C library. Most binaries take only a few seconds to build, so it's no big deal to build them several times a day, whenever a source file changes. The C library can take several tens of minutes or more to build—and it almost never changes.
dependencies	This target simply prints the names of the opt packages on which this opt package depends. The dependencies target is used by the elw script to build the complete list of opt packages needed for a project.

The Project Directory

Previous sections explained the contents of the Embedded Linux Workshop. This section explains the contents of the project directory, which contains the files that are specific to a particular project you may be building. The project directory is normally named after the project it contains. For instance, if you're using the Embedded Linux Workshop to build a router, your project directory might be named router.

The project directory contains the following files and directories.

File/Directory	Description
BUILD	The BUILD file contains a number that's incremented every time you build the project. This helps you keep track of different copies of the media.
arch and opt	These directories have the same layout as their counterparts in the Embedded Linux Workshop directory structure, and they serve the same purpose. You would put any code that's specific to the current project in these directories.
config	The config file is a piece of Perl code that configures the Embedded Linux Workshop for the project. It's described in detail in the next section.
obj	All the output of the Embedded Linux Workshop finds its way into the obj directory. It contains the root filesystem, the kernel, and the image that needs to make its way to the boot media.

The *config* file

Running elw --newproject zug at the command line produces the following output:

```
Building project zug:
#mkdir -p zug/obj
#mkdir -p zug/opt
#mkdir -p zug/arch/i386/opt
#mkdir -p zug/arch/i386/src/kernel
#touch zug/arch/i386/src/kernel/linux_directory_goes_here
#mkdir -p zug/mnt
```

Within the root of the new project is a file named config. The config file configures the Embedded Linux Workshop for the current project. Let's look at it piece by piece.

```
######################################################################
# Configuration for zug
# [NOTE: this file configures your project.  You must modify it as]
# [NOTE: necessary for your project.                              ]
######################################################################

$STYLE="syslinux";
```

The --newproject option defaults to the SYSLINUX style. Much of the following discussion is dependent on the SYSLINUX style. If you're using a different style, look at the source code for that style for more information on its needs.

```
# Initial Ram Disk
# ----------------
$INITRDSZ=10240;                        # Size (512 byte)
$INITRDINODES=1024;                     # inodes
```

These variables size the root filesystem.

```
# Disk image attributes
# -----------------------
$DISK_BLOCKS=1440;                              # 1K blocks of media
```

This one sizes the boot media. There are 1440 1KB blocks on a 1.44MB 3$1/2$-inch floppy disk.

```
# Application info
# -----------------------------------------
$APP_NAME="zug";
$APP_SNAM="zug";
$APP_VERS="0.0.1";
$APP_ROOT="/dev/fd0";                           # A 1.44mb floppy size
```

The $APP_ROOT variable is important because the boot script will attempt to mount its contents at boot time so it can get to the configuration information.

```
# Options required for this software package
# ------------------------------------------
@OPT=("zug");
@OPT=(@OPT,"bash");

# Debug packages
# --------------
@OPT=(@OPT,"fdisk");
@OPT=(@OPT,"strace");
@OPT=(@OPT,"vi");
```

The @OPT variable contains the packages that are specific to this project. The debug packages take some room, so they should be left out of the production image. Note that the elw script will find the packages, whether they're in the Embedded Linux Workshop directories or within the project's directories. If they're in both, the project's directory takes precedence.

```
# Devices for this package
# -----------------------
$DEV="ttyS0 ttyS1 ttyS2 ttyS3";
```

Your project may or may not need these devices. They're listed here mainly so you can see how to add devices to your final image. Use or remove them as you like.

The Build Process

As mentioned earlier in this chapter, building a project using the Embedded Linux Workshop is quite straightforward. Once you have all the software in the correct directories, the debugging cycle is quite simple:

1. Make a change to a piece of source code.
2. Choose Build Binaries from the Embedded Linux Workshop main menu.

3. Choose Build Image from the Embedded Linux Workshop main menu.

4. Choose Build Floppy from the Embedded Linux Workshop main menu.

5. Boot the floppy.

6. If you find a bug, go to step 1.

7. Ship it.

Terminology

Architecture

In the world of the Embedded Linux Workshop, an *architecture* defines a specific application and kernel binary type. For example, if your product is based on an ARM7 without an MMU running in little-endian mode, and you decide to statically link your applications against the uClibc library, your architecture may be named arm7-little-uClibc-static. You can name the architecture anything that makes sense to you. For instance, the architecture that comes with the ELW is named i386 for the Intel 80386 and compatible processors running applications that are dynamically linked with the glibc library.

Target

The actual files created by the ELW. These may be disk images or a series of files to install on a machine.

Target Processor

The ELW can cross-compile source into object code for different processors if the tool chain (compiler, linker, and so on) for that processor is installed.

Target Style

The type of target to create. A SYSLINUX disk image, a LILO disk image, a MILO disk image, etc. Most target styles have multiple suboptions. For instance, the SYSLINUX target style can create different disk image sizes, and can create upgrade files.

8

Static Application Example: Minicom

WHEN YOU'RE DONE WITH THIS EXAMPLE, you'll have a floppy disk that turns an x86-based computer (80386 and above) with a keyboard, VGA monitor, and floppy disk drive into a dumb serial terminal. We'll use Minicom, a serial communications application that comes with most Linux distributions, but we'll download all the software in this example from the Internet to show how easy it is.

This procedure takes somewhere between a half hour and two hours, depending on your hardware and experience—after you have the three files you need from the Internet. Before beginning this procedure, make sure that you have the following:

- 110MB free disk space in the filesystem you're going to use for this project
- An Internet connection
- A floppy disk
- A Linux computer with the ability to compile x86 binaries

Procedure

The procedure outlined in this chapter uses the components shown in the following table.

Component	Description
Linux 2.2 kernel	By the time you read this, the 2.4 kernel will be available and somewhat bug free. You may want to use the 2.4 kernel instead of the 2.2 kernel. If you do, you may have to modify the following procedure somewhat.
Minicom	Minicom is a great little serial communications utility. Because it's a simple application, anyone with a standard PC can use and test it. If you want to use a different application in the following procedure, you can do so, but remember that the procedure will need to change somewhat to accommodate that application.
SYSLINUX	The procedure uses SYSLINUX to boot the floppy disk. If you prefer, you can use GRUB or LILO.

Create the Directory

You should create a directory for each of your projects so that the files that comprise each project are kept in a well-defined place.

It's best to keep the source code for the components of your project along with the project itself. For instance, in the following steps you'll download the Linux kernel, Minicom, and SYSLINUX. But what happens if you make some changes to your copy today, and then you need to upgrade to new versions three years from now? You'll need the original source code to create patches to the new versions. Because it's so important to the Linux community at large, even three years from now you'll be able to download the sources for the exact version of the kernel you used with this procedure. However, you may not be able to get old versions of Minicom or SYSLINUX. It really depends on whether the maintainer of each package keeps all the old versions.

For this procedure, begin by creating a directory called `eminicom` to store the Minicom software. Then change to that directory in preparation for downloading Minicom:

```
mkdir eminicom
cd eminicom
```

Download Minicom

Minicom is a serial communications program originally written by Miquel van Smoorenburg. It's a lot like the old MS-DOS programs PROComm and Telix, which were used by many people in the days before the Internet to connect to bulletin board systems with a serial modem. It can also be used to connect a PC to devices such as routers and switches for initial configuration.

Minicom is a powerful program with a lot of configuration options. Help is available using the Alt+A Z key sequence. It will be helpful to read the man page for Minicom on the system on which you build the floppy disk, to familiarize yourself with Minicom's features. For instance, a Minicom configuration file could be added that enables Minicom to save its dial list to the floppy disk, so the dial list would be kept through reboot cycles.

Download the source code for Minicom from `www.pp.clinet.fi/~walker/ minicom.html`. If it's not there, use `www.freshmeat.net` to find it. If you have trouble downloading it, use `http://ftpsearch.lycos.com` to search for the filename, and then pick a site near you to download from. At the time of this writing, the latest version was 1.83.0.

Caution: Be careful when downloading files that end in `.gz` with Netscape. You should shift-click or right-click and Save As when attempting to download the files in this section. See the Netscape documentation for more information.

If you want to build a boot floppy for some other simple, single-binary application, you could download that application instead.

Download SYSLINUX

The documentation for SYSLINUX describes it like this:

What SYSLINUX Is

SYSLINUX is a boot loader for the Linux operating system which operates off an MS-DOS/Windows FAT filesystem. It is intended to simplify first-time installation of Linux, and for creation of rescue and other special-purpose boot disks.

SYSLINUX can be used, when properly set up, [to] completely eliminate the need for distribution of raw diskette images for boot floppies. A SYSLINUX floppy can be manipulated using standard MS-DOS (or any other OS that can access an MS-DOS filesystem) tools once it has been created.

What SYSLINUX Is Not

SYSLINUX is probably not suitable as a general purpose boot loader. It can only boot Linux from a FAT filesystem, and not, for example, ext2. Since a native Linux implementation will typically use ext2, another boot loader (e.g. LILO) is probably more suitable. In a system which actually contains DOS or Windows, LOADLIN may be simpler to use. However, SYSLINUX has shown itself to be quite useful in a number of special-purpose applications.

Download the latest version of SYSLINUX from `ftp://ftp.kernel.org/` `pub/linux/utils/boot/syslinux`. At the time of this writing, the latest version was 1.48. It's also possible to use GRUB or LILO, but SYSLINUX is a bit easier.

Download the Linux Kernel

Download the current production Linux kernel from `ftp://ftp.kernel.org/` `pub/linux/kernel`. At the time of this writing, the latest version was 2.2.19. It doesn't really matter which version of the kernel you use for this exercise. Anything from version 2.0 through 2.4+ should work just fine.

Untar the Files

Use the following commands to untar the `minicom` and `SYSLINUX` files and the Linux kernel:

```
tar xzf minicom-1.83.0.src.tar.gz
tar xzf syslinux-1.48.tar.gz
tar xzf linux-2.2.15.tar.gz
```

If you're using different versions, substitute the correct filenames in the commands above. When you're done, there will be a new directory named `linux`.

Tip: When untarring, change `xzf` to `xvzf` if you want to see the files that are created.

Caution: Be very careful not to blow away your current sources if you already have a `linux` directory. Normally, as soon as I untar a kernel I rename it to `linux-x.y.z`. On more than one occasion, I've untarred a newly downloaded kernel source tree and blown away another kernel I was already working on. Be careful!

Modify the Minicom Source

You have to make a few small changes to the source code for Minicom to make sure that it works properly in your mini-environment. Begin by changing to the Minicom source directory:

```
cd minicom-1.83.0/src
```

You need to modify the Makefile so that a static executable is produced. When you compile an application on a modern Linux system, it creates a dynamic executable that needs shared libraries for common functions such as `read()`, `write()`, and `printf()`. The whole point of this exercise is to create a static embedded application; this way, you don't have to worry about creating the shared libraries and setting them up so they'll work at runtime.

Look for the line that begins with `minicom:` and add `-static` somewhere on the next line. This single switch causes all the code necessary to run the application to be contained in the single executable. For instance, if the line says this:

```
$(CC) $(LFLAGS) -o minicom $(MOBJS) $(LIBS)
```

change it to look like this:

```
$(CC) -static $(LFLAGS) -o minicom $(MOBJS) $(LIBS)
```

Next, you need to remove a Minicom security feature that's unnecessary in this embedded application. In `minicom.c`, remove the entire `if` clause that contains the string `"You don't exist. Go away."` If this logic is not removed, Minicom will bail out when execution gets to this point. Since you don't have to be concerned with permissions and correct users in your embedded environment, it's safe to simply remove this logic.

Now make the `Minicom` executable file:

```
make
```

If everything goes well, you'll end up with a static executable file called `minicom`. You can make sure it's static with the `ldd` command:

```
$ ldd src/minicom
    libc.so.6 => /lib/libc.so.6 (0x4001e000)
    /lib/ld-linux.so.2 => /lib/ld-linux.so.2 (0x40000000)
```

Change directories back to the root of your project (`eminicom`) and create a blank initrd image by using the `dd` command:

```
cd ../..
dd if=/dev/zero of=fs bs=1k count=600
```

This command creates a file with 600 1KB blocks in it. Each block is filled with zeros. It's important to create this file from scratch each time because you want it to compress as much as possible. If you just keep using the same file over and over again, blocks that really have no data in them wouldn't compress well because they no longer are filled with only zeros. (When files are deleted, the contents of these files are still left inside the initrd.)

Create and Mount the Filesystem

Now you're ready to create the filesystem in the `fs` file. We'll use the e2fs filesystem because it's the best-tested filesystem in Linux:

```
mkfs.ext2 ./fs
```

Tip: You have a choice of several filesystem types for your root filesystem. The choice usually boils down to ext2 or minix. I typically use the ext2 filesystem, although the minix filesystem is quite a bit smaller.

Now mount the filesystem. Linux `mount` is pretty good at determining the filesystem type from the filesystem itself. If it has a problem, you may need to tell it what filesystem type it's dealing with, using the `-t` option.

```
mount -o loop fs /mnt
```

Create the Devices

You're ready to create the special files needed for your embedded environment. You must use the `-a` option of the `cp` command so that the directory entries are copied but the files themselves are not.

```
mkdir -p /mnt/dev
(cd /dev && cp -a console full kmem loop0 loop1 mem null port ram0 ram1 tty tty0
tty1 tty2 ttyS0 ttyS1 ttyS2 ttyS3 urandom zero /mnt/dev)
(cd /mnt/dev && ln -s /proc/kcore core)
(cd /mnt/dev && ln -s ram1 ram)
```

Now, create the `terminfo` for the console. This file contains the definitions of escape sequences for the console for operations such as clearing the screen and drawing lines:

```
cp -P /usr/share/terminfo/l/linux /mnt
```

Copy the Minicom Executable

Copy the Minicom executable to the `initrd` filesystem and name it `/linuxrc`:

```
cp minicom-1.83.0/src/minicom /mnt/linuxrc
```

You name the executable `/linuxrc` in your filesystem because that's the name of the script (or program in this case) that the Linux kernel will run when it's done booting. You might expect to name it `init` instead. But since you're using the `initrd` feature of the Linux kernel to load your application into memory, you must name it `linuxrc`, since that's what Linux expects when starting an `initrd` process.

Set the Root Directory

Test the setup by running the `linuxrc` program with `/mnt` set as the root directory. This way, you know that `/linuxrc` runs in the same environment it will run with on your device:

```
chroot /mnt /linuxrc
```

`chroot` runs the command specified by the third parameter, using the directory specified in the second parameter as its root directory. The command has no access to any files on the computer other than those under the specified root directory. The reason you run `/linuxrc` instead of `/mnt/linuxrc` is that the `chroot` happens before the execution of the command, and once the `chroot` happens the `linuxrc` file is then in the root of the new directory structure.

If everything goes okay, the Minicom program should start. If you're adventurous, you could attach a modem and put Minicom through its paces. To exit Minicom, press Ctrl+A X.

Compress the Filesystem

Now, unmount the `initrd` filesystem and compress it as much as possible (the `-9` option sacrifices speed for better compression):

```
umount /mnt
gzip -9 fs
```

Configure the Kernel

Change to the kernel directory:

```
cd linux
```

Configure the kernel using the `make menuconfig` command. The following options are based on a 2.2 Intel kernel; your kernel configuration may be a bit different. Turn off all options except the following:

Processor Type and features

386 processor family

1GB Maximum Physical Memory

General setup

Kernel support for ELF binaries

Block Devices

Normal PC floppy disk support

Enhanced IDE/MFM/RLL disk/CD-ROM/tape/floppy support

RAM disk support

Initial RAM disk (initrd) support

Character devices

Virtual Terminal

Support for console on virtual terminal

Standard/generic (dumb) serial support

Filesystems

DOS FAT fs support

MSDOS fs support

Second extended fs support

Console drivers

VGA text console

Build the kernel with the following command:

```
make dep && make bzImage
```

We use the "and" continuation (&&) instead of the semicolon (;) so that the second make won't happen if the first fails. I've never seen make dep fail when building the kernel, but this is good practice for all long software builds with more than one make. This way, if an error occurs in one of the makes, the subsequent makes won't even start, leaving you with any error messages still on the screen. We don't need to make any modules for this kernel, but if we did, I'd simply add it to the command line like this:

```
make dep && make bzImage && make modules
```

Build the Boot Floppy

Change back to the root directory of your project:

```
cd ..
```

Insert a floppy disk into the drive. We'll assume it's /dev/fd0 (/dev/fd0H1440).

The rest of this procedure assumes that you're using a $3^1/2$-inch floppy of 1.44MB capacity. If this assumption is incorrect, change the commands accordingly.

Perform a low-level format of the floppy disk. If you're sure the floppy is already formatted for 1.44MB, you can safely skip this step:

```
fdformat /dev/fd0H1440
```

Create an MS-DOS filesystem on the floppy disk and mount the floppy as an MS-DOS disk:

```
mkfs.msdos /dev/fd0
mount -t msdos /dev/fd0 /mnt
```

The mkfs.msdos command has a couple of parameters that you can tweak to get more room. If you're really pressed for space, add -f 1 to reduce the number of FAT tables to one.

Now copy the compressed kernel, the initrd filesystem, and the SYSLINUX MS-DOS floppy boot loader system file to the floppy disk:

```
cp linux/arch/i386/boot/bzImage /mnt
cp fs.gz /mnt
cp syslinux-1.48/ldlinux.sys /mnt
cat > /mnt/syslinux.cfg
LABEL linux
KERNEL bzimage
APPEND initrd=fs.gz
```

End the cat command with Ctrl+D. This command creates the syslinux.cfg file on the floppy disk.

Tip: Of course, you can use a more powerful editor such as `vi` or `emacs` to create this file, but for demonstration purposes this is the simplest way to describe how to create the file. For a lot more information about what can go in this file, see the `syslinux.doc` file in the SYSLINUX distribution.

Unmount the floppy disk, make it bootable, and use the `sync` command to make sure that all writes are synchronized to the floppy:

```
umount /mnt
syslinux-1.48/syslinux /dev/fd0
sync
```

Wait until the command prompt reappears. Then remove the floppy disk from your build machine and boot your test bed machine with it. If all goes well, Minicom should appear within a few seconds of booting.

Troubleshooting

There are several potential pitfalls you may run into while following this procedure. Some of them are covered in this section.

/usr/share/terminfo/l/linux **May Be Wrong**

If you're not running on Red Hat 6.2, your `terminfo` database may not be in `/usr/share`. If this is the case, find out where the `terminfo` database is and substitute that path for `/usr/share/terminfo/l/linux` everywhere you see it in the procedure.

You Need */dev/console*

Probably the least obvious thing about creating a bootable Linux floppy disk is the fact that you absolutely need the `/dev/console` device in your `initrd` filesystem because the kernel specifically attempts to open it before calling `/linuxrc`. If it doesn't exist, the `initrd` filesystem won't load, and the kernel will panic.

The *LABEL* **Statement in** *syslinux.cfg* **Must Be** *linux*

If you choose to call it something else, you must have a `DEFAULT` statement, or the user will have to type the name at boot time. See the `syslinux.doc` file in the SYSLINUX distribution for more information about the `syslinux.cfg` file.

Exiting from Your Application Panics the Kernel

The `initrd` filesystem was designed to be a short weigh-station in the boot process. All the kernel designers intended for you to do was load a kernel module or two (for SCSI drivers, for example), and then exit. The kernel would then mount the real root device and boot the user-mode part of the operating system.

You use the `initrd` filesystem differently here—your entire application runs out of it. Because of that, it's important to prevent the user from exiting the application. If that happens, the user gets a message like this:

```
hda:driver not present
VFS: Cannot open root device 03:01
Kernel panic: VFS: Unable to mount root fs on 03:01
```

Use *chroot* to Test on Your Build Machine

When your build machine is running the same processor as your target, you have several additional debug tricks available to you. One of the handiest is the `chroot` trick.

During the build process, you'll create a root filesystem image that the target machine will boot from. Once that image is created, it can be mounted using a loopback device. You can then use the `chroot` command to change a subshell's root directory to the mounted filesystem. Any commands you type in the subshell will be limited to using only files within the filesystem image you created. This is quite handy for checking to make sure that your software generally works before committing it to the target device. For instance, if you're missing a dynamic library, and you run a command that requires it, the command will error out.

Some things won't work, however. For instance, any command that relies on the `/proc` filesystem will fail. This is because the `/proc` file system is not available to the `chroot`ed environment.

9

Testing and Debugging

DEBUGGING AN EMBEDDED SYSTEM CAN BE A DAUNTING TASK. Developing software on a personal computer is easy by comparison—there's an operating system under your software to catch unexpected events, a screen to display debug messages, and a keyboard and mouse with which you can give your software input. Your embedded device may not have any of these; you may have only a little LED that your software can make blink—or you may not even have that!

From the beginning, you need to design your embedded application with diagnostics. If you don't, chances are that you'll eventually be faced with a little dead box and no way to know what happened. You'll wonder whether it will happen again—and then it will. This gives developers nightmares.

This chapter looks at several obvious (and some less obvious) tips and techniques for speeding the development and increasing the "debugability" of your embedded Linux device.

Test on Your Host Computer as Much as Possible

The target computer is a fun toy, and once it starts working, it seems to be the natural place to do all of your testing. After all, that's where the software has to run eventually—why not test it there?

That reasoning is invalid. You should test as much of your software as possible on your *host* computer system. If your host is running a different processor, modify your Makefiles so that the software can be built for your host or target. If your software depends on hardware that can only be found in the target, you can still test a lot of your code on the host by #ifdef-ing out the parts of the code that actually need the target's hardware.

Testing your software on your host is important for these reasons:

- **Access to debugging tools**

  You probably have better debugging tools—and more control over them—on your host computer than on your target computer. The host computer is probably a desktop computer running Linux. On it you probably have a large array of great software development tools—not just the compiler tool chain, but debuggers, debug libraries, memory bounds–checking libraries, tools such as strace, and so on. Chances are that many of these tools won't fit on your target box; they may not even have been ported to the processor you're using. But that doesn't mean that you can't *use* them. Compiling your software on your host machine allows you to use this array of tools for debugging your code—once you're satisfied with your changes, you can recompile the code for the target.

- **Simpler debugging cycle**

  The debugging cycle almost certainly will require considerably less effort on your host than on your target. The less time it takes you to start testing code that you have just changed, the better—especially if you're like me, and prefer to change a small bit of code and then run it, then change more small bits and run them. Your host computer probably compiles code for itself just as fast as it compiles code for your target; but once it's compiled, you don't need to move it anywhere—you can just run it where it is. It may take you several minutes (or longer) to move the code to the target, just to find out that you've made a mistake and have to repeat the whole process.

Of course, you do need to do some testing on your target, and the target's environment may be very different from the host's, not only in terms of hardware, but also the runtime environment—C libraries, other libraries, utility programs, and so on. If you go too long without moving the development code to the target computer, you may waste a lot of time backtracking because you made some incorrect assumptions about the target environment. This is especially true in the very beginning of a project, when you're new to the environment—the first order of business should be to get the hardware up and running, and then test your software on it at least once a day.

Sometimes it just doesn't make sense for you to debug your software on your host machine. For instance, if you're implementing a driver for hardware that can only exist on your target, you obviously can't do much beyond developing the stub code on your host machine. You may also want to steer clear of testing any "dangerous" software on your host machine. For instance, any software that, as part of its functionality, creates a new filesystem on the first partition of the first hard drive it sees should not be tested on your host machine—even if you believe that the dangerous code path cannot be reached. You may be correct when you originally think it, but as you test and debug your software, you may accidentally activate the wrong code path and blow away your machine.

Debugging Tools

Every software programmer develops a quiver of tools that he or she brings to bear on current projects. The tools described in the following sections are some that I've found very useful for software development. This is by no means a complete list of tools that can be used for building and debugging software, but getting to know at least these tools will help you develop Linux software more quickly and effectively.

VMware Workstation

VMware, Inc. describes VMware Workstation like this:

> VMware Workstation allows completely independent installations of oper-
> ating systems on a single machine. Multiple instances of Windows or
> Linux can run side by side. Each machine is equivalent to a PC, since it
> has a complete, unmodified operating system, a unique network address,
> and a full complement of hardware devices.

In essence, VMware Workstation allows you to run multiple operating systems at the same time on your x86 host computer. If your target happens to be an x86, this feature is extremely handy. You don't have to move any software to your target computer until it's time to actually test any hardware that you can't install into your host machine. VMware Workstation may also be useful if you're *not* targeting an x86-based machine. You can use VMware for much of the day-to-day development process, requiring less recompiling to the target architecture to do integration testing. Remember, keeping everything on one computer can be a great time-saver and make you a much more effective developer.

I use VMware Workstation extensively. My current development platform is a Dell Inspiron 7500 laptop computer. On it, I run (don't look) Windows 2000 as the host (VMware term) operating system. On another partition, I have an install of Red Hat Linux that I boot under Windows using VMware Workstation. Using Samba, I'm able to easily share files between the operating systems. I also run an X server for Windows 2000, so my X sessions appear like any other Windows application.

By the way—if you haven't already burned this book after reading the above—the reason that I run Windows 2000 as my main OS is so I can make use of the "hiber-nate" facility. With it, I can shut down my computer for days at a time—it draws no power. I can then restart the computer and have all my windows open to exactly where I was when I left off. All of my xterm sessions are still there, sitting right where I left them. If I was in the middle of inserting text in vi, I can go right back to doing that.

I used VMware extensively while developing the Embedded Linux Workshop in this book. With it, I don't need a target computer, and can develop completely on one box. ELW's build scripts build floppy images, which I boot using a new instance of VMware Workstation. This way, I can compile the target application, build the floppy image, and boot the image—all within two minutes. You can also use hard drive images. This way, an entire hard drive is mapped to a single file in your filesystem. This makes it hard for your test system to mess up your real hard disk partitions.

If you do decide to use VMware Workstation, make sure that your machine has enough horsepower. My 500 MHz 128MB Dell is a little underpowered for the job, especially if I have a lot of Windows applications open.

chroot

Sometimes booting VMware is too much of a hassle, or perhaps you're having trouble with libraries and your target machine doesn't boot at all. If your host and target are running the same hardware, or you're simply testing your software on the same hardware as your host, you can uncompress and mount your root image as a loop filesystem (`mount -o loop`) and then `chroot` to it. Doing this gives you *almost* the same environment that you'll get when running on different hardware. Any binaries you run will use the libraries of your target, the filesystem will be the same, and so on. This will suffice for testing many kinds of problems. You can even get fancy and copy tools like `strace` into the filesystem.

Some things won't be the same, however:

- **Kernel**

  You may be running a different version of Linux on your host than on your target. Depending on how different the versions are, the `chrooted` environment may not work at all on your host.

- **Boot code**

  Any necessary setup code that's normally done while your target hardware boots will have to be run manually when you start the `chrooted` environment.

- **/proc**

  You can't mount the `/proc` filesystem in your `chrooted` environment, so any software that relies on it will have difficulty.

- **Network connections**

  The networking facilities are not part of the filesystem, so they're visible in the `chrooted` environment.

- **System V IPC**

  Because the System V Inter Process Communication structures (shared memory, message queues, and semaphores) don't live in the filesystem, they're visible to the `chrooted` environment.

User Mode Linux

Somewhere between `chroot` and VMware is *User Mode Linux*. User Mode Linux enables you to set up a complete Linux kernel and runtime environment within the confines of a user mode Linux process.

It's a little more difficult to set up than the `chroot` example described earlier, but most of the mentioned restrictions are lifted. For more information, see `http://user-mode-linux.sourceforge.net/`.

strace

`strace` is a utility that should be in every Linux developer's bag of tricks, whether or not you're developing an embedded device. Many times, there's no quicker way to track down why a program is failing than to run it under `strace`. `strace` displays to `stderr` all of the system calls (along with their parameters and return values) that a program uses during execution. Since a program typically does a lot of system calls, there can be a lot of output—much of it useless to the problem at hand. But if you know what to look for, the interesting stuff can be priceless.

Let's look at an example. I was recently developing a program called `wb.o`. I had just written a bunch of new code, and when I ran the software I got a segmentation fault like this:

```
[root@jllinux cadmin]# ./wb -e showmeminfo
Segmentation fault (core dumped)
```

To debug the problem, I had several choices:

- **Review all the code I'd changed, to try to find the mistake.** If it had been a while since I made the changes, or if I made a lot of them, this could take a while.

- **Add a bunch of debug `printf()`s to localize the problem.** Of course, this solution is fairly hit-or-miss and can take a while.

- **Rerun the program under `gdb`.** Since I hadn't compiled it with debug information, this would have been slow. Without `strace`, however, this would have probably been the quickest choice.

- **Rerun the code under `strace`.**

The output is shown below. Note that all the `old_mmap()` and `mprotect()` calls were removed from the output for brevity:

```
[root@jllinux cadmin]# strace ./wb -e showmeminfo
execve("./wb", ["./wb", "-e", "showmeminfo"], [/* 23 vars */]) = 0
stat("/etc/ld.so.cache", {st_mode=S_IFREG|0644, st_size=34774, ...}) = 0
open("/etc/ld.so.cache", O_RDONLY)      = 3
close(3)                                = 0
stat("/etc/ld.so.preload", 0xbfffffae0) = -1 ENOENT (No such file or directory)
open("/lib/libuClibc.so.1", O_RDONLY)   = 3
```

continues

Continued

```
read(3, "\177ELF\1\1\1\0\0\0\0\0\0\0\0\0\3\0\3\0\1\0\0\0\260\310"..., 4096) = 4096
close(3)                          = 0
open("/lib/ld-linux.so.1", O_RDONLY)     = 3
read(3, "\177ELF\1\1\1\0\0\0\0\0\0\0\0\0\3\0\3\0\1\0\0\0@\v\0\000"..., 4096) =
↦4096
close(3)                          = 0
munmap(0x40008000, 34774)         = 0
personality(PER_LINUX)            = 0
ioctl(1, TCGETS, {B9600 opost isig icanon echo ...}) = 0
open("/envi", O_RDONLY)           = 3
mremap(0x19000000, 4096, 8192, )      = 0x19000000
ioctl(3, TCGETS, 0xbffff9fc)              = -1 ENOTTY (Inappropriate ioctl for
↦device)
read(3, "# Embedded Linux Netdevice\n# Not"..., 512) = 512
read(3, "_BEG1=\"10.0.0.100\"\nexport DHCPD_"..., 512) = 43
read(3, "", 512)                  = 0
close(3)                          = 0
open("/CONFIG", O_RDONLY)             = -1 ENOENT (No such file or directory)
—- SIGSEGV (Segmentation fault) —-
+++ killed by SIGSEGV +++
```

Notice that the last thing that happens before the segmentation fault is the open()ing of the "/CONFIG" file—also notice that the open() failed. This ended up being a big clue—the code didn't deal with this failure case properly, and a null pointer was read. The whole process took two minutes from the time I saw the first Segmentation fault (core dumped) message. It would have taken a lot longer with any of the other methods I mentioned earlier.

ltrace

Similar to strace, ltrace traces library calls. It displays both the parameters passed to the function and the return value. Combined with strace, it's extremely useful for debugging problems when the source code is not readily available, or when debugging with gdb is too much of a hassle.

gdb and Other Debuggers

It's usually worth spending time figuring out how to use gdb (the GNU Debugger) or another debugger with your target hardware, especially if you're going to spend a lot of time on a project. gdb can save you a lot of time and energy when you have a particularly nasty bug.

If your target device has a console, you can run gdb directly on the device as usual, simply by compiling using the -g option and running the executable under gdb. If your target doesn't have a console, you can still use gdb by connecting your host to your target through the serial port. You can then use gdb remotely from your host.

printf() and *printk()*

Eventually, you have to stop developing on your host machine and start developing on the target. On the target, you will usually be pretty limited in the debug tools available to you. You may get lucky and have debug hardware that allows you to single-step your software using gdb or some other debugger, but this won't always be the case. Eventually, you'll get to the point where you need to debug code running at full speed in a limited environment. The best way to do that is to pepper the code with printf() or printk() (depending on whether you're debugging application code or kernel code). Using this debug style is pretty straightforward, but it's sometimes missed as the easiest way to localize a problem.

syslog()

Related to printf() and printk(), described in the preceding section, is syslog(). syslog() sends a string to an error-logging process on the current machine or another machine. It's especially handy when you're debugging a problem on a target machine on which you don't have a command shell. You can instruct syslog() to send debug messages to your host machine, where you can readily view them.

LEDs

What do you do if you don't have a display or serial port or network connection? Hopefully, you have one or more LEDs that you can light up using software. This is a painful way to debug software, and can be quite time-consuming—but it has been done, and if there is no better way...

expect

Most serious software development projects result in two sets of software: the application software that answers the problem at hand, and a test suite that verifies the application software. The test suite is usually in the form of numerous small programs and scripts, each of which checks an individual aspect of the application software, returning a pass/fail result. Many of these little programs and scripts are written so that, as bugs are squashed, they test for the reappearance of the bug. As the project progresses, the developer often runs the test suite to make sure the software is not sliding backward. This is called *regression testing*.

It quickly becomes cumbersome to run each test individually, so they must somehow be scripted. However, the script normally runs on a machine separate from the target machine in an embedded environment, so how can you get the tests to run and verify the results over a serial or network link?

One powerful tool for scripting these tests and verifying their results is expect. From the man page:

> expect is a program that "talks" to other interactive programs according to a script. Following the script, expect knows what can be expected from a program and what the correct response should be. An interpreted language provides branching and high-level control structures to direct the dialogue. In addition, the user can take control and interact directly when desired, afterward returning control to the script.

Using expect, you can build a script that connects to the embedded box, runs each diagnostic test and verifies each result. If a problem occurs, you can leave the connection open and run the test or check the status yourself.

10

Embedded Linux Success Stories

Currently Linux is embedded in several successful products, with more being announced every day. This chapter briefly introduces a few of the more interesting products that are actually on the market that use Linux as the operating system.

One of the interesting things to realize about these products is that Linux is relegated to a mere footnote or not mentioned at all in the product literature—there's no "Linux Inside" sticker stamped on the side. From a marketing standpoint, the fact that Linux is used in the product is a non-issue.

TiVo (*www.tivo.com*)

The first commercially successful embedded Linux device is TiVo, which lets you digitally record television programs and play them back whenever you want.

TiVo works like this: Late at night, it uses its built-in modem to call a central TiVo server, which contains all of the programming information for the next few days. You are then able to tell TiVo which program(s) you want to record. It records the program(s) and stores the data on a built-in hard drive, and you can then play back the recorded show(s) whenever you want.

TiVo also allows you to "pause" live television. That is, you can press a key on your remote, and the current program will begin recording. You can then press the play button to begin watching the recorded show. Similarly, you can "rewind" live TV. The TiVo is always recording the last 30 minutes of whatever you're watching, so you can always rewind whatever you're watching... neat.

Specifications

While the TiVo is an embedded Linux device, it doesn't suffer from the space restraints of many other embedded devices. There's a lot of room for software on the hard drive, where the recording software itself resides. Even so, the TiVo designers chose some interesting hardware. Much of the following information came from the TiVo FAQ (`http://www.tivofaq.com/hack/faq.html`).

- **Processor:** IBM PowerPC 403GCX
- **Video decoder/scaler:** Philips SAA7114H
- **Sound processor for analog TV signals:** Miconas MSP 3430Ga4
- **Video encoder YUV to NTSC or PAL:** Philips SAA7120H
- **MPEG audio/video decoder:** IBM CS22PFJ22C
- **MPEG-II clock synthesizer:** ICS MK2745-265
- **V.90/K56flex/V.34 modem data pump:** Conexant RP336LD
- **Micro controller for modem chip:** Rockwell P39X
- **16 bit DSP:** Analog Devices ADSP-2183
- **MPEG-II video encoder:** Sony CXD1922Q

Diamond Riocar (*www.riohome.com*)

The Riocar audio player is a digital music player that you mount inside your car's dashboard just like a regular car radio. It can store more than 1,000 hours of MP3 music—that's enough music to keep you entertained if you ever decide to circumnavigate the world in your car. Two and a half times.

The music files are loaded from your PC using your serial port, a USB cable, or Ethernet. An FM tuner is also available.

Specifications

Much of this information comes from the Linux Devices review at `http://www.linuxdevices.com/articles/AT5630105143.html`.

- **Processor:** Intel StrongARM 200 MHz
- **HD space:** Two $2^1/2$-inch laptop drives
- **Memory:** 12MB
- **Flash:** 1MB
- **DSP:** Phillips SAA7705H
- **Pre-amps:** Burr Brown

Axis Network Camera (*www.axis.com*)

The Axis Network Camera is a video camera and Web server all contained in a package no bigger than a standard handheld camcorder. Plug one side into your LAN, point the other side at an object to display on the network, and voilà, instant video server.

Specifications

Axis has a good Web site for their products. The information below is from the datasheet on the Axis 2120 Web camera at
`http://www.axis.com/documentation/datasheet/2120/2120ds.pdf`.

- **Processor:** AXIS ETRAX-100
- **Memory:** 16MB
- **Flash:** 4MB
- **Image compression:** AXIS ARTPEC-1

Summary

In addition to commercial applications, there are many research projects, machine shop automation projects, and so on that embed Linux into hardware other than the ubiquitous desktop form factor. For instance, take a look at the data acquisition system controller used by NASA to hunt hurricanes (see `http://lidar.wff.nasa.gov/sra/lj98/`).

IV

Appendixes

GNU General Public License

T HE FOLLOWING IS A VERBATIM COPY OF THE GNU General Public License (GPL), formatted to fit this work. It is not included as part of this work because this work is covered under the GPL—indeed, this work is *not* covered under the GPL. The GPL is merely included here as a reference to the reader.

GNU GENERAL PUBLIC LICENSE

Version 2, June 1991

Copyright (C) 1989, 1991 Free Software Foundation, Inc.
59 Temple Place, Suite 330, Boston, MA 02111-1307 USA

Everyone is permitted to copy and distribute verbatim copies
of this license document, but changing it is not allowed.

Preamble

The licenses for most software are designed to take away your freedom to share and change it. By contrast, the GNU General Public License is intended to guarantee your freedom to share and change free software—to make sure the software is free for all its users. This General Public License applies to most of the Free Software Foundation's software and to any other program whose authors commit to using it.

(Some other Free Software Foundation software is covered by the GNU Library General Public License instead.) You can apply it to your programs, too.

When we speak of free software, we are referring to freedom, not price. Our General Public Licenses are designed to make sure that you have the freedom to distribute copies of free software (and charge for this service if you wish), that you receive source code or can get it if you want it, that you can change the software or use pieces of it in new free programs; and that you know you can do these things.

To protect your rights, we need to make restrictions that forbid anyone to deny you these rights or to ask you to surrender the rights. These restrictions translate to certain responsibilities for you if you distribute copies of the software, or if you modify it.

For example, if you distribute copies of such a program, whether gratis or for a fee, you must give the recipients all the rights that you have. You must make sure that they, too, receive or can get the source code. And you must show them these terms so they know their rights.

We protect your rights with two steps: (1) copyright the software, and (2) offer you this license which gives you legal permission to copy, distribute and/or modify the software.

Also, for each author's protection and ours, we want to make certain that everyone understands that there is no warranty for this free software. If the software is modified by someone else and passed on, we want its recipients to know that what they have is not the original, so that any problems introduced by others will not reflect on the original authors' reputations.

Finally, any free program is threatened constantly by software patents. We wish to avoid the danger that redistributors of a free program will individually obtain patent licenses, in effect making the program proprietary. To prevent this, we have made it clear that any patent must be licensed for everyone's free use or not licensed at all.

The precise terms and conditions for copying, distribution and modification follow.

TERMS AND CONDITIONS FOR COPYING, DISTRIBUTION AND MODIFICATION

0. This License applies to any program or other work which contains a notice placed by the copyright holder saying it may be distributed under the terms of this General Public License. The "Program", below, refers to any such program or work, and a "work based on the Program" means either the Program or any derivative work under copyright law: that is to say, a work containing the Program or a portion of it, either verbatim or with modifications and/or translated into another language. (Hereinafter, translation is included without limitation in the term "modification".) Each licensee is addressed as "you".

Activities other than copying, distribution and modification are not covered by this License; they are outside its scope. The act of running the Program is not restricted, and the output from the Program is covered only if its contents constitute a work based on the Program (independent of having been made by running the Program). Whether that is true depends on what the Program does.

1. You may copy and distribute verbatim copies of the Program's source code as you receive it, in any medium, provided that you conspicuously and appropriately publish on each copy an appropriate copyright notice and disclaimer of warranty; keep intact all the notices that refer to this License and to the absence of any warranty; and give any other recipients of the Program a copy of this License along with the Program.

You may charge a fee for the physical act of transferring a copy, and you may at your option offer warranty protection in exchange for a fee.

2. You may modify your copy or copies of the Program or any portion of it, thus forming a work based on the Program, and copy and distribute such modifications or work under the terms of Section 1 above, provided that you also meet all of these conditions:

- **a)** You must cause the modified files to carry prominent notices stating that you changed the files and the date of any change.

- **b)** You must cause any work that you distribute or publish, that in whole or in part contains or is derived from the Program or any part thereof, to be licensed as a whole at no charge to all third parties under the terms of this License.

- **c)** If the modified program normally reads commands interactively when run, you must cause it, when started running for such interactive use in the most ordinary way, to print or display an announcement including an appropriate copyright notice and a notice that there is no warranty (or else, saying that you provide a warranty) and that users may redistribute the program under these conditions, and telling the user how to view a copy of this License. (Exception: if the Program itself is interactive but does not normally print such an announcement, your work based on the Program is not required to print an announcement.)

These requirements apply to the modified work as a whole. If identifiable sections of that work are not derived from the Program, and can be reasonably considered independent and separate works in themselves, then this License, and its terms, do not apply to those sections when you distribute them as separate works. But when you distribute the same sections as part of a whole which is a work based on the Program, the distribution of the whole must be on the terms of this License, whose permissions for other licensees extend to the entire whole, and thus to each and every part regardless of who wrote it.

Thus, it is not the intent of this section to claim rights or contest your rights to work written entirely by you; rather, the intent is to exercise the right to control the distribution of derivative or collective works based on the Program.

In addition, mere aggregation of another work not based on the Program with the Program (or with a work based on the Program) on a volume of a storage or distribution medium does not bring the other work under the scope of this License.

3. You may copy and distribute the Program (or a work based on it, under Section 2) in object code or executable form under the terms of Sections 1 and 2 above provided that you also do one of the following:

- **a)** Accompany it with the complete corresponding machine-readable source code, which must be distributed under the terms of Sections 1 and 2 above on a medium customarily used for software interchange; or,

- **b)** Accompany it with a written offer, valid for at least three years, to give any third party, for a charge no more than your cost of physically performing source distribution, a complete machine-readable copy of the corresponding source code, to be distributed under the terms of Sections 1 and 2 above on a medium customarily used for software interchange; or,

- **c)** Accompany it with the information you received as to the offer to distribute corresponding source code. (This alternative is allowed only for noncommercial distribution and only if you received the program in object code or executable form with such an offer, in accord with Subsection b above.)

The source code for a work means the preferred form of the work for making modifications to it. For an executable work, complete source code means all the source code for all modules it contains, plus any associated interface definition files, plus the scripts used to control compilation and installation of the executable. However, as a special exception, the source code distributed need not include anything that is normally distributed (in either source or binary form) with the major components (compiler, kernel, and so on) of the operating system on which the executable runs, unless that component itself accompanies the executable.

If distribution of executable or object code is made by offering access to copy from a designated place, then offering equivalent access to copy the source code from the same place counts as distribution of the source code, even though third parties are not compelled to copy the source along with the object code.

4. You may not copy, modify, sublicense, or distribute the Program except as expressly provided under this License. Any attempt otherwise to copy, modify, sublicense or distribute the Program is void, and will automatically terminate your rights under this License. However, parties who have received copies, or rights, from you under this License will not have their licenses terminated so long as such parties remain in full compliance.

5. You are not required to accept this License, since you have not signed it. However, nothing else grants you permission to modify or distribute the Program or its derivative works. These actions are prohibited by law if you do not accept this License. Therefore, by modifying or distributing the Program (or any work based on the Program), you indicate your acceptance of this License to do so, and all its terms and conditions for copying, distributing or modifying the Program or works based on it.

6. Each time you redistribute the Program (or any work based on the Program), the recipient automatically receives a license from the original licensor to copy, distribute or modify the Program subject to these terms and conditions. You may not impose any further restrictions on the recipients' exercise of the rights granted herein. You are not responsible for enforcing compliance by third parties to this License.

7. If, as a consequence of a court judgment or allegation of patent infringement or for any other reason (not limited to patent issues), conditions are imposed on you (whether by court order, agreement or otherwise) that contradict the conditions of this License, they do not excuse you from the conditions of this License. If you cannot distribute so as to satisfy simultaneously your obligations under this License and any other pertinent obligations, then as a consequence you may not distribute the Program at all. For example, if a patent license would not permit royalty-free redistribution of the Program by all those who receive copies directly or indirectly through you, then the only way you could satisfy both it and this License would be to refrain entirely from distribution of the Program.

If any portion of this section is held invalid or unenforceable under any particular circumstance, the balance of the section is intended to apply and the section as a whole is intended to apply in other circumstances.

It is not the purpose of this section to induce you to infringe any patents or other property right claims or to contest validity of any such claims; this section has the sole purpose of protecting the integrity of the free software distribution system, which is implemented by public license practices. Many people have made generous contributions to the wide range of software distributed through that system in reliance on consistent application of that system; it is up to the author/donor to decide if he or she is willing to distribute software through any other system and a licensee cannot impose that choice.

This section is intended to make thoroughly clear what is believed to be a consequence of the rest of this License.

8. If the distribution and/or use of the Program is restricted in certain countries either by patents or by copyrighted interfaces, the original copyright holder who places the Program under this License may add an explicit geographical distribution limitation excluding those countries, so that distribution is permitted only in or among countries not thus excluded. In such case, this License incorporates the limitation as if written in the body of this License.

9. The Free Software Foundation may publish revised and/or new versions of the General Public License from time to time. Such new versions will be similar in spirit to the present version, but may differ in detail to address new problems or concerns.

Each version is given a distinguishing version number. If the Program specifies a version number of this License which applies to it and "any later version", you have the option of following the terms and conditions either of that version or of any later version published by the Free Software Foundation. If the Program does not specify a version number of this License, you may choose any version ever published by the Free Software Foundation.

10. If you wish to incorporate parts of the Program into other free programs whose distribution conditions are different, write to the author to ask for permission. For software which is copyrighted by the Free Software Foundation, write to the Free Software Foundation; we sometimes make exceptions for this. Our decision will be guided by the two goals of preserving the free status of all derivatives of our free software and of promoting the sharing and reuse of software generally.

NO WARRANTY

11. BECAUSE THE PROGRAM IS LICENSED FREE OF CHARGE, THERE IS NO WARRANTY FOR THE PROGRAM, TO THE EXTENT PERMITTED BY APPLICABLE LAW. EXCEPT WHEN OTHERWISE STATED IN WRITING THE COPYRIGHT HOLDERS AND/OR OTHER PARTIES PROVIDE THE PROGRAM "AS IS" WITHOUT WARRANTY OF ANY KIND, EITHER EXPRESSED OR IMPLIED, INCLUDING, BUT NOT LIMITED TO, THE IMPLIED WARRANTIES OF MERCHANTABILITY AND FITNESS FOR A PARTICULAR PURPOSE. THE ENTIRE RISK AS TO THE QUALITY AND PERFORMANCE OF THE PROGRAM IS WITH YOU. SHOULD THE PROGRAM PROVE DEFECTIVE, YOU ASSUME THE COST OF ALL NECESSARY SERVICING, REPAIR OR CORRECTION.

12. IN NO EVENT UNLESS REQUIRED BY APPLICABLE LAW OR AGREED TO IN WRITING WILL ANY COPYRIGHT HOLDER, OR ANY OTHER PARTY WHO MAY MODIFY AND/OR REDISTRIBUTE THE PROGRAM AS PERMITTED ABOVE, BE LIABLE TO YOU FOR DAMAGES, INCLUDING ANY GENERAL, SPECIAL, INCIDENTAL OR CONSEQUENTIAL DAMAGES ARISING OUT OF THE USE OR INABILITY TO USE THE PROGRAM (INCLUDING BUT NOT LIMITED TO LOSS OF DATA OR DATA BEING RENDERED INACCURATE OR LOSSES SUSTAINED BY YOU OR THIRD PARTIES OR A FAILURE OF THE PROGRAM TO OPERATE WITH ANY OTHER PROGRAMS), EVEN IF SUCH HOLDER OR OTHER PARTY HAS BEEN ADVISED OF THE POSSIBILITY OF SUCH DAMAGES.

END OF TERMS AND CONDITIONS

How to Apply These Terms to Your New Programs

If you develop a new program, and you want it to be of the greatest possible use to the public, the best way to achieve this is to make it free software which everyone can redistribute and change under these terms.

To do so, attach the following notices to the program. It is safest to attach them to the start of each source file to most effectively convey the exclusion of warranty; and each file should have at least the "copyright" line and a pointer to where the full notice is found.

one line to give the program's name and a brief idea of what it does.
Copyright (C) *yyyy name of author*

This program is free software; you can redistribute it and/or modify it under the terms of the GNU General Public License as published by the Free Software Foundation; either version 2 of the License, or (at your option) any later version.

This program is distributed in the hope that it will be useful, but WITHOUT ANY WARRANTY; without even the implied warranty of MERCHANTABILITY or FITNESS FOR A PARTICULAR PURPOSE. See the GNU General Public License for more details.

You should have received a copy of the GNU General Public License along with this program; if not, write to the Free Software Foundation, Inc., 59 Temple Place, Suite 330, Boston, MA 02111-1307 USA

Also add information on how to contact you by electronic and paper mail.

If the program is interactive, make it output a short notice like this when it starts in an interactive mode:

Gnomovision version 69, Copyright (C) *year name of author*
Gnomovision comes with ABSOLUTELY NO WARRANTY; for details type 'show w'. This is free software, and you are welcome to redistribute it under certain conditions; type 'show c' for details.

The hypothetical commands 'show w' and 'show c' should show the appropriate parts of the General Public License. Of course, the commands you use may be called something other than 'show w' and 'show c'; they could even be mouse-clicks or menu items—whatever suits your program.

You should also get your employer (if you work as a programmer) or your school, if any, to sign a "copyright disclaimer" for the program, if necessary. Here is a sample; alter the names:

Yoyodyne, Inc., hereby disclaims all copyright interest in the program ' Gnomovision ' (which makes passes at compilers) written by James Hacker.

signature of Ty Coon, 1 April 1989
Ty Coon, President of Vice

This General Public License does not permit incorporating your program into proprietary programs. If your program is a subroutine library, you may consider it more useful to permit linking proprietary applications with the library. If this is what you want to do, use the GNU Library General Public License instead of this License.

B

GNU Lesser General Public License

THE FOLLOWING IS A VERBATIM COPY OF THE GNU Lesser General Public License (LGPL), which is generally used as a copyright for library code that can be linked with proprietary code. It is formatted to fit this work. It is not included as part of this work because this work is covered under the LGPL—indeed, this work is *not* covered under the LGPL. The LGPL is merely included here as a reference to the reader.

GNU LESSER GENERAL PUBLIC LICENSE

Version 2.1, February 1999

Copyright (C) 1991, 1999 Free Software Foundation, Inc.
59 Temple Place, Suite 330, Boston, MA 02111-1307 USA
Everyone is permitted to copy and distribute verbatim copies
of this license document, but changing it is not allowed.

[This is the first released version of the Lesser GPL. It also counts
as the successor of the GNU Library Public License, version 2, hence
the version number 2.1.]

Preamble

The licenses for most software are designed to take away your freedom to share and change it. By contrast, the GNU General Public Licenses are intended to guarantee your freedom to share and change free software—to make sure the software is free for all its users.

This license, the Lesser General Public License, applies to some specially designated software packages—typically libraries—of the Free Software Foundation and other authors who decide to use it. You can use it too, but we suggest you first think carefully about whether this license or the ordinary General Public License is the better strategy to use in any particular case, based on the explanations below.

When we speak of free software, we are referring to freedom of use, not price. Our General Public Licenses are designed to make sure that you have the freedom to distribute copies of free software (and charge for this service if you wish); that you receive source code or can get it if you want it; that you can change the software and use pieces of it in new free programs; and that you are informed that you can do these things.

To protect your rights, we need to make restrictions that forbid distributors to deny you these rights or to ask you to surrender these rights. These restrictions translate to certain responsibilities for you if you distribute copies of the library or if you modify it.

For example, if you distribute copies of the library, whether gratis or for a fee, you must give the recipients all the rights that we gave you. You must make sure that they, too, receive or can get the source code. If you link other code with the library, you must provide complete object files to the recipients, so that they can relink them with the library after making changes to the library and recompiling it. And you must show them these terms so they know their rights.

We protect your rights with a two-step method: (1) we copyright the library, and (2) we offer you this license, which gives you legal permission to copy, distribute and/or modify the library.

To protect each distributor, we want to make it very clear that there is no warranty for the free library. Also, if the library is modified by someone else and passed on, the recipients should know that what they have is not the original version, so that the original author's reputation will not be affected by problems that might be introduced by others.

Finally, software patents pose a constant threat to the existence of any free program. We wish to make sure that a company cannot effectively restrict the users of a free program by obtaining a restrictive license from a patent holder. Therefore, we insist that any patent license obtained for a version of the library must be consistent with the full freedom of use specified in this license.

Most GNU software, including some libraries, is covered by the ordinary GNU General Public License. This license, the GNU Lesser General Public License, applies to certain designated libraries, and is quite different from the ordinary General Public License. We use this license for certain libraries in order to permit linking those libraries into non-free programs.

When a program is linked with a library, whether statically or using a shared library, the combination of the two is legally speaking a combined work, a derivative of the original library. The ordinary General Public License therefore permits such linking only if the entire combination fits its criteria of freedom. The Lesser General Public License permits more lax criteria for linking other code with the library.

We call this license the "Lesser" General Public License because it does Less to protect the user's freedom than the ordinary General Public License. It also provides other free software developers Less of an advantage over competing non-free programs. These disadvantages are the reason we use the ordinary General Public License for many libraries. However, the Lesser license provides advantages in certain special circumstances.

For example, on rare occasions, there may be a special need to encourage the widest possible use of a certain library, so that it becomes a de-facto standard. To achieve this, non-free programs must be allowed to use the library. A more frequent case is that a free library does the same job as widely used non-free libraries. In this case, there is little to gain by limiting the free library to free software only, so we use the Lesser General Public License.

In other cases, permission to use a particular library in non-free programs enables a greater number of people to use a large body of free software. For example, permission to use the GNU C Library in non-free programs enables many more people to use the whole GNU operating system, as well as its variant, the GNU/Linux operating system.

Although the Lesser General Public License is Less protective of the users' freedom, it does ensure that the user of a program that is linked with the Library has the freedom and the wherewithal to run that program using a modified version of the Library.

The precise terms and conditions for copying, distribution and modification follow. Pay close attention to the difference between a "work based on the library" and a "work that uses the library". The former contains code derived from the library, whereas the latter must be combined with the library in order to run.

TERMS AND CONDITIONS FOR COPYING, DISTRIBUTION AND MODIFICATION

0. This License Agreement applies to any software library or other program which contains a notice placed by the copyright holder or other authorized party saying it may be distributed under the terms of this Lesser General Public License (also called "this License"). Each licensee is addressed as "you".

A "library" means a collection of software functions and/or data prepared so as to be conveniently linked with application programs (which use some of those functions and data) to form executables.

The "Library", below, refers to any such software library or work which has been distributed under these terms. A "work based on the Library" means either the Library or any derivative work under copyright law: that is to say, a work containing the Library or a portion of it, either verbatim or with modifications and/or translated straightforwardly into another language. (Hereinafter, translation is included without limitation in the term "modification".)

"Source code" for a work means the preferred form of the work for making modifications to it. For a library, complete source code means all the source code for all modules it contains, plus any associated interface definition files, plus the scripts used to control compilation and installation of the library.

Activities other than copying, distribution and modification are not covered by this License; they are outside its scope. The act of running a program using the Library is not restricted, and output from such a program is covered only if its contents constitute a work based on the Library (independent of the use of the Library in a tool for writing it). Whether that is true depends on what the Library does and what the program that uses the Library does.

1. You may copy and distribute verbatim copies of the Library's complete source code as you receive it, in any medium, provided that you conspicuously and appropriately publish on each copy an appropriate copyright notice and disclaimer of warranty; keep intact all the notices that refer to this License and to the absence of any warranty; and distribute a copy of this License along with the Library.

You may charge a fee for the physical act of transferring a copy, and you may at your option offer warranty protection in exchange for a fee.

2. You may modify your copy or copies of the Library or any portion of it, thus forming a work based on the Library, and copy and distribute such modifications or work under the terms of Section 1 above, provided that you also meet all of these conditions:

- **a)** The modified work must itself be a software library.
- **b)** You must cause the files modified to carry prominent notices stating that you changed the files and the date of any change.
- **c)** You must cause the whole of the work to be licensed at no charge to all third parties under the terms of this License.
- **d)** If a facility in the modified Library refers to a function or a table of data to be supplied by an application program that uses the facility, other than as an argument passed when the facility is invoked, then you must make a good faith effort to ensure that, in the event an application does not supply such function or table, the facility still operates, and performs whatever part of its purpose remains meaningful.

(For example, a function in a library to compute square roots has a purpose that is entirely well-defined independent of the application. Therefore, Subsection 2d requires that any application-supplied function or table used by this function must be optional: if the application does not supply it, the square root function must still compute square roots.)

These requirements apply to the modified work as a whole. If identifiable sections of that work are not derived from the Library, and can be reasonably considered independent and separate works in themselves, then this License, and its terms, do not apply to those sections when you distribute them as separate works. But when you distribute the same sections as part of a whole which is a work based on the Library, the distribution of the whole must be on the terms of this License, whose permissions for other licensees extend to the entire whole, and thus to each and every part regardless of who wrote it.

Thus, it is not the intent of this section to claim rights or contest your rights to work written entirely by you; rather, the intent is to exercise the right to control the distribution of derivative or collective works based on the Library.

In addition, mere aggregation of another work not based on the Library with the Library (or with a work based on the Library) on a volume of a storage or distribution medium does not bring the other work under the scope of this License.

3. You may opt to apply the terms of the ordinary GNU General Public License instead of this License to a given copy of the Library. To do this, you must alter all the notices that refer to this License, so that they refer to the ordinary GNU General Public License, version 2, instead of to this License. (If a newer version than version 2 of the ordinary GNU General Public License has appeared, then you can specify that version instead if you wish.) Do not make any other change in these notices.

Once this change is made in a given copy, it is irreversible for that copy, so the ordinary GNU General Public License applies to all subsequent copies and derivative works made from that copy.

This option is useful when you wish to copy part of the code of the Library into a program that is not a library.

4. You may copy and distribute the Library (or a portion or derivative of it, under Section 2) in object code or executable form under the terms of Sections 1 and 2 above provided that you accompany it with the complete corresponding machine-readable source code, which must be distributed under the terms of Sections 1 and 2 above on a medium customarily used for software interchange.

If distribution of object code is made by offering access to copy from a designated place, then offering equivalent access to copy the source code from the same place satisfies the requirement to distribute the source code, even though third parties are not compelled to copy the source along with the object code.

5. A program that contains no derivative of any portion of the Library, but is designed to work with the Library by being compiled or linked with it, is called a "work that uses the Library". Such a work, in isolation, is not a derivative work of the Library, and therefore falls outside the scope of this License.

However, linking a "work that uses the Library" with the Library creates an executable that is a derivative of the Library (because it contains portions of the Library), rather than a "work that uses the library". The executable is therefore covered by this License. Section 6 states terms for distribution of such executables.

When a "work that uses the Library" uses material from a header file that is part of the Library, the object code for the work may be a derivative work of the Library even though the source code is not. Whether this is true is especially significant if the work can be linked without the Library, or if the work is itself a library. The threshold for this to be true is not precisely defined by law.

If such an object file uses only numerical parameters, data structure layouts and accessors, and small macros and small inline functions (ten lines or less in length), then the use of the object file is unrestricted, regardless of whether it is legally a derivative work. (Executables containing this object code plus portions of the Library will still fall under Section 6.)

Otherwise, if the work is a derivative of the Library, you may distribute the object code for the work under the terms of Section 6. Any executables containing that work also fall under Section 6, whether or not they are linked directly with the Library itself.

6. As an exception to the Sections above, you may also combine or link a "work that uses the Library" with the Library to produce a work containing portions of the Library, and distribute that work under terms of your choice, provided that the terms permit modification of the work for the customer's own use and reverse engineering for debugging such modifications.

You must give prominent notice with each copy of the work that the Library is used in it and that the Library and its use are covered by this License. You must supply a copy of this License. If the work during execution displays copyright notices, you must include the copyright notice for the Library among them, as well as a reference directing the user to the copy of this License. Also, you must do one of these things:

- **a)** Accompany the work with the complete corresponding machine-readable source code for the Library including whatever changes were used in the work (which must be distributed under Sections 1 and 2 above); and, if the work is an executable linked with the Library, with the complete machine-readable "work that uses the Library", as object code and/or source code, so that the user can modify the Library and then relink to produce a modified executable containing the modified Library. (It is understood that the user who changes the contents of definitions files in the Library will not necessarily be able to recompile the application to use the modified definitions.)

- **b)** Use a suitable shared library mechanism for linking with the Library. A suitable mechanism is one that (1) uses at run time a copy of the library already present on the user's computer system, rather than copying library functions into the executable, and (2) will operate properly with a modified version of the library, if the user installs one, as long as the modified version is interface-compatible with the version that the work was made with.

- **c)** Accompany the work with a written offer, valid for at least three years, to give the same user the materials specified in Subsection 6a, above, for a charge no more than the cost of performing this distribution.

- **d)** If distribution of the work is made by offering access to copy from a designated place, offer equivalent access to copy the above specified materials from the same place.

- **e)** Verify that the user has already received a copy of these materials or that you have already sent this user a copy.

For an executable, the required form of the "work that uses the Library" must include any data and utility programs needed for reproducing the executable from it. However, as a special exception, the materials to be distributed need not include anything that is normally distributed (in either source or binary form) with the major components (compiler, kernel, and so on) of the operating system on which the executable runs, unless that component itself accompanies the executable.

It may happen that this requirement contradicts the license restrictions of other proprietary libraries that do not normally accompany the operating system. Such a contradiction means you cannot use both them and the Library together in an executable that you distribute.

7. You may place library facilities that are a work based on the Library side-by-side in a single library together with other library facilities not covered by this License, and distribute such a combined library, provided that the separate distribution of the work based on the Library and of the other library facilities is otherwise permitted, and provided that you do these two things:

- **a)** Accompany the combined library with a copy of the same work based on the Library, uncombined with any other library facilities. This must be distributed under the terms of the Sections above.

- **b)** Give prominent notice with the combined library of the fact that part of it is a work based on the Library, and explaining where to find the accompanying uncombined form of the same work.

8. You may not copy, modify, sublicense, link with, or distribute the Library except as expressly provided under this License. Any attempt otherwise to copy, modify, sublicense, link with, or distribute the Library is void, and will automatically terminate your rights under this License. However, parties who have received copies, or rights, from you under this License will not have their licenses terminated so long as such parties remain in full compliance.

9. You are not required to accept this License, since you have not signed it. However, nothing else grants you permission to modify or distribute the Library or its derivative works. These actions are prohibited by law if you do not accept this License. Therefore, by modifying or distributing the Library (or any work based on the Library), you indicate your acceptance of this License to do so, and all its terms and conditions for copying, distributing or modifying the Library or works based on it.

10. Each time you redistribute the Library (or any work based on the Library), the recipient automatically receives a license from the original licensor to copy, distribute, link with or modify the Library subject to these terms and conditions. You may not impose any further restrictions on the recipients' exercise of the rights granted herein. You are not responsible for enforcing compliance by third parties with this License.

11. If, as a consequence of a court judgment or allegation of patent infringement or for any other reason (not limited to patent issues), conditions are imposed on you (whether by court order, agreement or otherwise) that contradict the conditions of this License, they do not excuse you from the conditions of this License. If you cannot distribute so as to satisfy simultaneously your obligations under this License and any other pertinent obligations, then as a consequence you may not distribute the Library at all. For example, if a patent license would not permit royalty-free redistribution of the Library by all those who receive copies directly or indirectly through you, then the only way you could satisfy both it and this License would be to refrain entirely from distribution of the Library.

If any portion of this section is held invalid or unenforceable under any particular circumstance, the balance of the section is intended to apply, and the section as a whole is intended to apply in other circumstances.

It is not the purpose of this section to induce you to infringe any patents or other property right claims or to contest validity of any such claims; this section has the sole purpose of protecting the integrity of the free software distribution system which is implemented by public license practices. Many people have made generous contributions to the wide range of software distributed through that system in reliance on consistent application of that system; it is up to the author/donor to decide if he or she is willing to distribute software through any other system and a licensee cannot impose that choice.

This section is intended to make thoroughly clear what is believed to be a consequence of the rest of this License.

12. If the distribution and/or use of the Library is restricted in certain countries either by patents or by copyrighted interfaces, the original copyright holder who places the Library under this License may add an explicit geographical distribution limitation excluding those countries, so that distribution is permitted only in or among countries not thus excluded. In such case, this License incorporates the limitation as if written in the body of this License.

13. The Free Software Foundation may publish revised and/or new versions of the Lesser General Public License from time to time. Such new versions will be similar in spirit to the present version, but may differ in detail to address new problems or concerns.

Each version is given a distinguishing version number. If the Library specifies a version number of this License which applies to it and "any later version", you have the option of following the terms and conditions either of that version or of any later version published by the Free Software Foundation. If the Library does not specify a license version number, you may choose any version ever published by the Free Software Foundation.

14. If you wish to incorporate parts of the Library into other free programs whose distribution conditions are incompatible with these, write to the author to ask for permission. For software which is copyrighted by the Free Software Foundation, write to the Free Software Foundation; we sometimes make exceptions for this. Our decision will be guided by the two goals of preserving the free status of all derivatives of our free software and of promoting the sharing and reuse of software generally.

NO WARRANTY

15. BECAUSE THE LIBRARY IS LICENSED FREE OF CHARGE, THERE IS NO WARRANTY FOR THE LIBRARY, TO THE EXTENT PERMITTED BY APPLICABLE LAW. EXCEPT WHEN OTHERWISE STATED IN WRITING THE COPYRIGHT HOLDERS AND/OR OTHER PARTIES PROVIDE THE LIBRARY "AS IS" WITHOUT WARRANTY OF ANY KIND, EITHER EXPRESSED OR IMPLIED, INCLUDING, BUT NOT LIMITED TO, THE IMPLIED WARRANTIES OF MERCHANTABILITY AND FITNESS FOR A PARTICULAR PURPOSE. THE ENTIRE RISK AS TO THE QUALITY AND PERFORMANCE OF THE LIBRARY IS WITH YOU. SHOULD THE LIBRARY PROVE DEFECTIVE, YOU ASSUME THE COST OF ALL NECESSARY SERVICING, REPAIR OR CORRECTION.

16. IN NO EVENT UNLESS REQUIRED BY APPLICABLE LAW OR AGREED TO IN WRITING WILL ANY COPYRIGHT HOLDER, OR ANY OTHER PARTY WHO MAY MODIFY AND/OR REDISTRIBUTE THE LIBRARY AS PERMITTED ABOVE, BE LIABLE TO YOU FOR DAMAGES, INCLUDING ANY GENERAL, SPECIAL, INCIDENTAL OR CONSEQUENTIAL DAMAGES ARISING OUT OF THE USE OR INABILITY TO USE THE LIBRARY (INCLUDING BUT NOT LIMITED TO LOSS OF DATA OR DATA BEING RENDERED INACCURATE OR LOSSES SUSTAINED BY YOU OR THIRD PARTIES OR A FAILURE OF THE LIBRARY TO OPERATE WITH ANY OTHER SOFTWARE), EVEN IF SUCH HOLDER OR OTHER PARTY HAS BEEN ADVISED OF THE POSSIBILITY OF SUCH DAMAGES.

END OF TERMS AND CONDITIONS

How to Apply These Terms to Your New Libraries

If you develop a new library, and you want it to be of the greatest possible use to the public, we recommend making it free software that everyone can redistribute and change. You can do so by permitting redistribution under these terms (or, alternatively, under the terms of the ordinary General Public License).

To apply these terms, attach the following notices to the library. It is safest to attach them to the start of each source file to most effectively convey the exclusion of warranty; and each file should have at least the "copyright" line and a pointer to where the full notice is found.

one line to give the library's name and a brief idea of what it does.
Copyright (C) *year name of author*

This library is free software; you can redistribute it and/or modify it under the terms of the GNU Lesser General Public License as published by the Free Software Foundation; either version 2.1 of the License, or (at your option) any later version.

This library is distributed in the hope that it will be useful, but WITHOUT ANY WARRANTY; without even the implied warranty of MERCHANTABILITY or FITNESS FOR A PARTICULAR PURPOSE. See the GNU Lesser General Public License for more details.

You should have received a copy of the GNU Lesser General Public License along with this library; if not, write to the Free Software Foundation, Inc., 59 Temple Place, Suite 330, Boston, MA 02111-1307 USA

Also add information on how to contact you by electronic and paper mail.

You should also get your employer (if you work as a programmer) or your school, if any, to sign a "copyright disclaimer" for the library, if necessary. Here is a sample; alter the names:

Yoyodyne, Inc., hereby disclaims all copyright interest in the library 'Frob' (a library for tweaking knobs) written by James Random Hacker.

signature of Ty Coon, 1 April 1990
Ty Coon, President of Vice

That's all there is to it!

Booting from Flash Memory

C

SOMETIMES YOU CAN'T JUSTIFY THE TIME AND EXPENSE of developing a dedicated hardware platform for your embedded application. Perhaps the quantities are too small or the market is unproven. However, even under these circumstances you still don't want to ship a big klunky box with a hard drive. Hard drives wear out over time; they also draw lots of power and get very hot. Besides, customers know a PC when they see one. Fortunately, manufacturers are starting to produce PC-compatible computer systems with form factors that please embedded system designers. Some look like set-top boxes (think VCR), some are rack mountable. In the future, we'll even see some that look like a desktop hub or modem. However, the hard drive remains a problem.

Currently, flash memory is the best substitute for a hard drive in an embedded device. It has several advantages over a hard drive: It's faster, it draws much less power, it produces less heat than a hard drive, and it has no moving parts. Unlike a hard drive, the processor can directly address the bits stored in flash memory just like RAM, making execution in place (XIP) possible, thereby reducing the overall RAM requirements. However, the disadvantages of flash memory may be prohibitive: It's much more expensive than an equal amount of hard drive space; it has much less capacity; and, as you write to flash memories, they slowly wear out.

In 1994, M-Systems (www.m-sys.com) introduced the *DiskOnChip*, a small flash memory device that works like a small hard drive. It can plug directly into a properly equipped motherboard, or into an ISA card for development. The DiskOnChip comes in a variety of sizes ranging from 2MB to 512MB, and in a variety of packages—DIP, TSOP-II, or DIMM. Depending on your application, the DiskOnChip may be the perfect storage solution for smaller-run embedded Linux devices based on the x86 processor, for several reasons:

- It's relatively easy to use.
- Many motherboards intended for embedded applications support it.
- It's not much more expensive than plain flash chips.
- It comes with block drivers that make it look like a hard drive.
- You can boot Linux directly from it.

However, for the Open Source purist, the DiskOnChip has one really big disadvantage: The driver from M-Systems is not Open Source. If you use the driver improperly, you'll violate the GPL. It's possible to avoid this violation by installing the driver as a module at runtime with the `insmod` or `modprobe` command. By the time you read this, work should be complete on a completely Open Source MTD DiskOnChip driver in the 2.4 kernel. If you're using kernel 2.4 or above, you should look at the instructions for using the built-in drivers before using the drivers from M-Systems.

An alternative to DiskOnChip is *Compact Flash* (*CF*). A Compact Flash device looks like an ATA/IDE hard drive to Linux. Because of this, Linux can boot from it as easily as from a hard drive with no additional drivers. Compact Flash devices are also very inexpensive because of their use in a great number of consumer electronics such as digital cameras and MP3 players.

This appendix guides you through the process of building a custom Linux image and installing it on the DiskOnChip in such a way that you won't violate the GPL. The image will be bootable and you'll be able to distribute the hardware without any sort of spinning media—hard drive, floppy drive, or CD-ROM. We'll build the Minicom application discussed in Chapter 8—but it will boot from the DiskOnChip instead of the floppy disk drive.

Generally, there are two phases to generating a working embedded Linux device based on the DiskOnChip:

1. Building the DiskOnChip files.
2. Installing the files onto the DiskOnChip.

The following sections provide details on these procedures.

Building the DiskOnChip Files

This procedure uses the Embedded Linux Workshop presented in Chapter 7. We'll use the workshop to re-create our favorite example, the Minicom appliance (also used in Chapter 8).

1. Acquire root privileges for your machine, if you don't already have them. Because the Embedded Linux Workshop mounts and unmounts filesystems, there's really no way to run it except as root.

2. Download the Embedded Linux Workshop. It's available from `http://elw.sourceforge.net` or `ftp://elw.sourceforge.net/pub/elw/`. There are a lot of files to download if you want the full source to the ELW. However, for now you only need the workshop itself. It will be named `elw-X.Y.Z.tgz`, where `X.Y.Z` is the current version number. If you just want to experiment with the Embedded Linux Workshop, you won't need to download all the source code to all the packages. However, if you're targeting a non–x86 CPU or want to do more than fool around with the software, you'll have to download most of the Embedded Linux Workshop source code over time.

3. `cd /usr/local`

   Change to the `/usr/local` directory. This is the easiest place to install the Embedded Linux Workshop. If you decide to install it somewhere else, make sure that you point your `/usr/local/elw` symbolic link to the right place.

4. `tar xvzf /tmp/elw-X.Y.Z.tgz`

   Install the Embedded Linux Workshop into the `/usr/local` directory. The example command assumes that you downloaded the `elw X.Y.Z.tgz` tarball into the `/tmp` directory.

5. `rm -f elw && ln -s elw-X.Y.Z elw`

   Remove the old `elw` symbolic link and create a new one that points to the directory you just installed. If you need to revert to a previous version of the Embedded Linux Workshop, you can just point this symbolic link back to the old version.

6. `cd /usr/bin && rm -f elw && ln -s /usr/local/elw/bin/elw elw`

   Remove any old `/usr/bin/elw` link and create a new one that points to the `elw` script in the `elw` package.

7. `cd ~yourhome/projects`

   Change to the directory where you want your new project to live.

8. `elw --newproject minicom`

   Use the `elw` command installed in the previous steps to create the new project. Several directories and files are created within the new `minicom` directory.

9. `cd minicom/arch/i386/src`

   Change to the `src` directory.

10. `mkdir minicom`

    Create the `minicom` directory, in which you'll keep the source code for Minicom.

11. `mkdir DOC`

    Create the `DOC` directory (short for DiskOnChip), in which you'll keep the source code for the DiskOnChip driver.

12. `cd minicom`

    Change to the new `minicom` directory.

13. Download Minicom from `www.pp.clinet.fi/~walker/minicom.html`. If it's not there, use `www.freshmeat.net` to find it. If you have trouble downloading it, use `http://ftpsearch.lycos.com` to search for the filename; choose a site near you to download from. At the time of this writing, the latest version was 1.83.1.

14. `tar xzf minicom-1.83.1.src.tar.gz`

    Untar Minicom. (To see the files that are created, change `xzf` in the command to `xvzf`.)

15. `ln -s minicom-1.83.1 minicom`

    Create a symbolic link named `minicom` that points to `minicom-1.83.1`. This symlink will be used in the `opt/minicom/Makefile`; this way, if you decide to upgrade to a later version of Minicom in the future, you can just change the symbolic link to point to the new version.

16. `cd minicom/src`

    Change to the `minicom` source directory.

17. We have to make a small change to the source code for Minicom, to make sure that it works properly in our mini-environment. We'll remove a Minicom security feature that's unnecessary in our embedded application. In `minicom.c`, search for the line that reads as follows:

    `if (real_uid == 0 && dosetup == 0) {`

    Delete about 61 lines—up to, but not including the following line:

    `buf[0] = 0;`

    If these lines are not removed, Minicom will bail out at this point. Since we don't have to be concerned with permissions and correct users in our embedded environment, it's safe to simply remove this code.

    Save your changes.

18. `make`

    Make the `minicom` executable file. If everything goes well, you'll end up with an executable file called `minicom`.

19. `cd ../../../kernel`

    Change to the kernel source directory.

20. Download the current production Linux kernel from `ftp.kernel.org/pub/linux/kernel`.

    At the time of this writing, the latest version was 2.2.15. It shouldn't really matter which version of the kernel you use for this exercise; anything from version 2.0 through 2.4+ should work just fine. However, the binary-only DiskOnChip driver may have trouble with some kernels. It's best to use whichever kernel the DiskOnChip driver is compiled on. That may be difficult to do until you try it with one kernel and it complains.

21. `tar xzf linux-2.2.15.tar.gz`

    Untar the kernel. When you're done, there will be a new directory named `linux`.

    Normally, as soon as I untar a kernel I rename it to `linux-X.Y.Z` and create a symbolic link named `linux` back to it, so I'll know what it is later on. Be very careful not to blow away your current sources if you already have a `linux` directory. On more than one occasion I've untarred a newly downloaded kernel source tree and blown away another kernel I was already working on.

22. `cd ../DOC`

    Change to the DiskOnChip source directory, `DOC`.

23. Download the latest DiskOnChip drivers from M-System's Web site (`www.m-sys.com`). You may have to fill out a form to do this.

24. `tar xvf DOC_Linux4.2.1.tar`

    M-Systems is trying to be Linux-friendly, but as of this writing they haven't quite figured it out. Every time I test this step, M-Systems has changed the way their download works, so if the filename isn't right or what you get doesn't match the instructions, you're on your own. The package you get is put together in a non–Linux way. It's a tar file containing a `License.TXT` and a `tgz`. The `tgz` contains the actual driver code.

25. `tar xvzf driver*tgz`

    Untar the `tgz`. You'll get a new tree, the root of which should look something like `Linux_DOC_4.2.1`.

26. `cd Linux_DOC_4.2.1/driver`

    This directory contains the files we need. `README.kit` contains a detailed set of instructions for the Linux DiskOnChip driver. We're interested in section 3, the part that talks about compiling a loadable module.

27. `./create-standalone driver-patch ../../../kernel/linux`

    The `../../kernel/linux` directory should be the Linux directory you created earlier. This step is supposed to create a new directory named `doc-module` in the root of the Linux source tree—the driver files will end up in this new directory.

28. `[ -d doc-module ] && mv doc-module ../../../kernel/linux`

    This step fixes a bug in the `create-standalone` script. In the current driver version (as of this writing), the `doc-module` is created in the wrong place. This step puts it where it belongs—in the kernel source tree.

29. `./mknod_fl`

    This script creates all the device entries for the DiskOnChip in the `/dev` directory. You can't do anything with these devices until you've loaded the driver.

30. `[ -d /dev/msys ] && (cd /dev/msys && mv * .. && cd .. && rmdir msys)`

    The Embedded Linux Workshop expects the devices it uses to be in `/dev`, so we simply move the devices created in step 29 into the `/dev` directory.

31. `cd ../../../kernel/linux`

    Change to the kernel directory.

32. `make menuconfig`

    Configure the kernel using the `make menuconfig` command. The following options are based on a 2.2.15 Intel kernel; your kernel configuration may be a bit different. Turn these options on with an asterisk (*), not an M; everything else should be turned off to save space. You'll have to go into each of the top-level menus, even the ones not listed here, to make sure that they're off.

    Processor Type and features

    386 processor family

    1G Maximum Physical Memory

    Loadable module support

    Enable loadable module support

    General Setup

    Kernel support for ELF binaries

    Block Devices

    Normal PC floppy disk support

    RAM disk support

    Initial RAM disk (initrd) support

    Character devices

    Virtual Terminal

    Support for console on virtual terminal

    Standard/generic (dumb) serial support

Filesystems

DOS FAT fs support

MSDOS fs support

VFAT (Windows-95) fs support

/proc filesystem support

Second extended fs support

Console Drivers

VGA text console

33. `make dep && make bzImage`

Build the kernel. We use the "and" continuation (&&) instead of the semicolon (;) so that the second `make` won't happen if the first fails. I've never seen `make dep` fail when building the kernel, but this is good practice for all long software builds with more than one `make`. This way, if there's an error in one of the `makes`, the subsequent `makes` won't even start, leaving any error messages still on the screen. We don't need to make any modules for this kernel, but if we did, I'd simply add each module to the command line like this.

    ```
    make dep && make bzImage && make modules
    ```

34. `cd doc-module`

    Change to the directory created by the `create-standalone` script from the DiskOnChip distribution.

35. `make`

    Build the `doc.o` module.

36. `cd ~yourname/projects/minicom`

    Change back to the root directory of your project.

37. `mkdir -p opt/minicom/bin opt/minicom/etc/rc`

    Create the Minicom package directories.

38. Use the `cat` command to build the `Makefile`:

    ```
    cat > opt/minicom/Makefile

    everytime:

    binaries:
            @(cd ../../src/minicom/minicom/src && make)
            @cp -f ../../src/minicom/minicom/src/minicom bin
            @strip bin/minicom
            @strip --remove-section=.note --remove-section=.comment bin/minicom

    dependencies:

            @echo "libncurses"
    ```

Press Ctrl+D here.

In the Embedded Linux Workshop, each `opt` package can have a `Makefile`. The `Makefile` has three targets: `everytime`, `binaries`, and `dependencies`. The `everytime` target is normally not used. The `binaries` target is used to rebuild any binaries whose source has changed since the last build and then move those binaries into the `opt` package. Once in the package, the binaries are then stripped. Finally, the `dependencies` target lists any dependencies for the `opt` package. For instance, the `minicom` executable depends on the `ncurses` library. Obviously, you don't have to use the `cat` command to build the `Makefile`; it's just the most convenient way in this HOWTO.

Note that the indented lines are indented with a single tab.

39. Now we'll use the `cat` command to create the startup script for Minicom:

    ```
    cat > opt/minicom/etc/rc/S99minicom
    ```

    ```
    #!/bin/sh
    echo "Press a key for minicom..."
    read x
    minicom -s
    ```

    Press Ctrl+D here.

    The Embedded Linux Workshop comes complete with a set of startup scripts that work similarly to the Red Hat startup scripts. Each script in the `/etc/rc` directory that begins with the letter *S* is executed in increasing sort order. Naming a script `S99{something}` implies that it should be the last script to run and that it may not return to the caller.

    We use the `-s` option so Minicom will go directly into setup mode. It defaults to COM2; change that setting if necessary. In a real device, you would create a `minicom` configuration file and let it start directly. Also, in a real application we wouldn't force the user to press a key to start, but this way we can see any bootup error messages before Minicom erases them.

40. `chmod a+x opt/minicom/etc/rc/S99minicom`

    Make the script executable.

41. `mkdir -p opt/doc/modules opt/doc/etc/rc`

    Create the `doc` package directories.

42. Back to the `cat` command once more to create the DiskOnChip Makefile:

    ```
    cat > opt/doc/Makefile
    ```

    ```
    everytime:

    binaries:

        @cp -f ../../src/kernel/linux/doc-module/doc.o modules
    ```

Press Ctrl+D here.

By convention, we don't recompile any part of the kernel or libc—it just takes too long.

43. `cp -P /usr/share/terminfo/l/linux opt/minicom`

    Create the `terminfo` file for the console. This file contains the definitions of escape sequences for the console for operations such as clearing the screen and drawing lines.

44. Type the following commands:
    ```
    cat > opt/doc/etc/rc/P01doc
    #!/bin/sh
    insmod -f /modules/doc.o
    ```

    Press Ctrl+D here.

    Each script in the `/etc/rc` directory that begins with the letter *P* is executed in increasing sort order before the boot media (flash filesystem) is mounted. This is how we're able to load the DiskOnChip module before we ever try to reference it. We use the `-f` (force) option of `insmod` because the kernel version encoded in the DiskOnChip driver may not agree with the kernel version we use. This happens because we aren't compiling the DiskOnChip driver from scratch, since we don't have the source.

45. `chmod a+x opt/doc/etc/rc/P01doc`

    Make the script executable.

46. Modify the `config` file in the root of the project in the following ways:
    `$APP_ROOT="/dev/fla1";`

    After `@OPT=("minicom");` add the following new line:
    `@OPT=(@OPT,"doc");`

47. `elw`

    Run the `elw` command.

48. Choose the `Build binaries` option to build the binaries. Unless you take the time to download all the source files to the Embedded Linux Workshop, most of the binaries will fail to build. That's okay; the binaries that ship will work. You must rerun this option each time you make a change.

49. Choose the `Build image` option to build the Linux files and image.

Congratulations—you've just created a new embedded Linux disk image!

Files

The `Build image` menu entry created several new files in the `obj` subdirectory:

File	Description
`obj/image`	An image of the bootable 1.44 MB floppy disk. If you used the `dd` command to copy this file to a floppy disk, it would boot into Minicom.
`obj/imageroot/*`	Contains all the files used to build the `obj/image` file. These are the files that actually need to get to the DiskOnChip.
`obj/imageroot/banner.txt`	This file is displayed on the console as the image boots. The file is built once by the `elw--newproject` command. Once built, it can be modified to display what you want to see. The source of this file is in `mnt/banner.txt`.
`obj/imageroot/bzImage`	This file is the actual Linux kernel. It's copied directly from within the kernel you built in the preceding procedure.
`obj/imageroot/ldlinux.sys`	The meat of the SYSLINUX bootloader. It copies the kernel from the boot media into memory and then executes it.
`obj/imageroot/readme`	A short text file that tells what's on the image. It's built once by the `elw--newproject` command. Its source is in `mnt/readme`.
`obj/imageroot/rootfs.gz`	Contains the `initrd` filesystem. This is the runtime root filesystem of any ELW project. SYSLINUX uncompresses it into memory as it loads it from the boot media.
`obj/imageroot/syslinux.cfg`	Tells SYSLINUX how to boot the media. It's built once by the `elw--newproject` command. Normally you shouldn't have to change it; its source is in the `mnt/syslinux.cfg` file. Look to the SYSLINUX documentation for more information about this file.

Installing the Image or Files onto the DiskOnChip

There are many ways to move the files onto the DiskOnChip. Depending on what hardware you have available, you may have several options:

- Put all the files on a DOS-formatted floppy disk, boot the box with the DiskOnChip using the floppy, and then copy the files from the floppy to the DiskOnChip.

- Put all the files on a DOS hard disk partition, boot the box with the DiskOnChip using that partition, and then copy the files from the floppy to the DiskOnChip.

- Dispense with DOS entirely by recompiling the Linux kernel on the box with the DiskOnChip and a hard drive, including the DiskOnChip drivers from M-Systems. Once you do that, you can copy the files directly from Linux to the DiskOnChip.

- If your DiskOnChip box doesn't have a hard disk or floppy disk controller, you'll have to program the DiskOnChip on another machine, perhaps using the ISA DiskOnChip card from M-Systems. Once the DiskOnChip is programmed, you'll move it to the destination box.

This appendix assumes that you have available a motherboard with a DiskOnChip socket and an IDE hard drive. We'll move the files to a bootable DOS partition on the hard drive, and then reboot under DOS. It will then be a simple exercise to copy the files to the DiskOnChip and run `syslinux.com` to make the kernel bootable from the DiskOnChip.

Using a hard drive with MS-DOS, follow these steps:

1. Locate all the files you'll need to install your new embedded Linux application on the DiskOnChip:

    - All the files in the `obj/imageroot` directory.
    - The `syslinux.com` file. If you installed the Embedded Linux Workshop in the standard place, it'll be in this location:
      `/usr/local/elw/arch/i386/opt/syslinux/nomedia/syslinux.com`.

2. Install a hard drive with a DOS partition into the machine with the DiskOnChip. Microsoft Windows should also work well, if you prefer. In fact, Microsoft Windows may be easier to use, since you're going to have to copy files from the `obj/imageroot` directory onto the DOS partition, and you may want to use the network. If you don't have access to MS-DOS or Windows, you can use Linux. However, to do so requires that you install the M-Systems drivers into your kernel (or compile them as modules and `insmod` them).

3. Boot the machine using DOS. You may have to tweak the BIOS to allow you to boot from the hard drive.

4. Get the files from your build machine to the local hard drive.

   It's up to you how you do this—anything from FTP to the hard drive shuffle will work. I suggest thinking hard about how you're going to do this, since you're probably going to do it many, many times. The less time you spend moving files from point A to point B so you can test, the more time you can spend engineering and debugging. Figure that you'll probably rebuild the project at least 100 times for anything more than a trivial project.

5. Determine the drive letter of your DiskOnChip device. The following steps assume that it's D:, but it could be a different letter for you.

6. (Optional) Delete all the files on the root of the DiskOnChip. You may not need (or want!) to do this.

7. `copy C:\imageroot\*.* d:\`

   Copy all the files in the `obj/imageroot` to the root of the DiskOnChip drive, using the DOS `copy` command. This step assumes that the files are in the `C:\imageroot` directory of the hard drive and that the DiskOnChip was assigned drive letter D:.

8. `c:\syslinux d:`

   Make the DiskOnChip bootable with the `syslinux.com` command. The command in this step assumes that the `syslinux.com` program is in the root of drive C:.

9. Reboot, changing the BIOS so the machine boots from the DiskOnChip.

Summary

If all went well, you now have a machine that pretends to be a serial terminal. That's probably not what you want to do with your embedded device, but you can swap out Minicom with your own software and you're well on your way to building your own embedded Linux device.

D

Embedded Linux Resources

THERE ARE A LOT OF WEB SITES DEVOTED to using Linux within embedded devices. Besides having varying amounts of their own content, the sites mentioned in this chapter have links to a lot of other sites that have more specific information about targeted aspects of embedding Linux on devices.

This Book's Web Site:
www.EmbeddedLinuxBook.com

As of June 2001, the whole idea of embedding Linux into products is still young. There are many Web sites devoted to this concept, plenty of great ideas, many prototypes, and many product announcements—but only a few shipping products.

Companies such as Lineo are pouring research dollars into building the infrastructure required to effectively embed Linux into products. Great Open Source projects such as BusyBox, uClibc, and uClinux are thriving.

Every effort has been made to make this book stand on its own for several years and not be tied to a particular technology, but the march of time demands that this book's resources must continue to grow to keep up with changing technology. The Web site for the book will always be a place where you can find links to the latest information on how to embed Linux into your product.

Web Sites Devoted to Embedded Linux

The following sites are excellent resources for anyone who needs all the gory details on building and working with custom embedded Linux systems.

LinuxDevices.com (*www.LinuxDevices.com*)

In October 1999, LinuxDevices.com was launched. Calling themselves "the embedded Linux portal," LinuxDevices.com has some good information about using Linux in embedded applications. The site features news, articles, polls, forums, event and job listings, product information, and a links page.

All Linux Devices (*www.AllLinuxDevices.com*)

All Linux Devices describes itself as "Your Daily Source for Embedded Linux Information." The site posts articles and press releases directly related to embedded Linux. It features a talkback section, user contributions, and "triggers" that will email you when a categorized piece of news is posted to the site.

The Embedded Linux Consortium (*www.embedded-linux.org*)

The Embedded Linux Consortium describes itself as follows:

> The Embedded Linux Consortium (ELC) is a nonprofit, vendor-neutral trade association whose goal is the advancement and promotion of Linux throughout the embedded, applied, and appliance computing markets. Members contribute dues and participate in management, promotion, and implementation efforts, in return for a growing market opportunity for all.
>
> Their mission is simple:
> ...to make Linux a top operating system choice for developers designing embedded systems.

Index

VOICES THAT MATTER

VISIT OUR WEB SITE

WWW.NEWRIDERS.COM

On our web site, you'll find information about our other books, authors, tables of contents, and book errata. You will also find information about book registration and how to purchase our books, both domestically and internationally.

EMAIL US

Contact us at: **nrfeedback@newriders.com**

- If you have comments or questions about this book
- To report errors that you have found in this book
- If you have a book proposal to submit or are interested in writing for New Riders
- If you are an expert in a computer topic or technology and are interested in being a technical editor who reviews manuscripts for technical accuracy

Contact us at: **nreducation@newriders.com**

- If you are an instructor from an educational institution who wants to preview New Riders books for classroom use. Email should include your name, title, school, department, address, phone number, office days/hours, text in use, and enrollment, along with your request for desk/examination copies and/or additional information.

Contact us at: **nrmedia@newriders.com**

- If you are a member of the media who is interested in reviewing copies of New Riders books. Send your name, mailing address, and email address, along with the name of the publication or web site you work for.

BULK PURCHASES/CORPORATE SALES

If you are interested in buying 10 or more copies of a title or want to set up an account for your company to purchase directly from the publisher at a substantial discount, contact us at 800-382-3419 or email your contact information to corpsales@pearsontechgroup.com. A sales representative will contact you with more information.

WRITE TO US

New Riders Publishing
201 W. 103rd St.
Indianapolis, IN 46290-1097

CALL/FAX US

Toll-free (800) 571-5840
If outside U.S. (317) 581-3500
Ask for New Riders
FAX: (317) 581-4663

New Riders

RELATED NEW RIDERS TITLES

ISBN: 0735709211
800 pages
US $49.99

MySQL

Paul DuBois

MySQL teaches readers how to use the tools provided by the MySQL distribution, by covering installation, setup, daily use, security, optimization, maintenance, and troubleshooting. It also discusses important third-party tools, such as the Perl DBI and Apache/PHP interfaces that provide access to MySQL.

ISBN: 0735710546
500 pages
US $44.99

MySQL and Perl for the Web

Paul DuBois

This book teaches readers the best method for providing information services through the use of Perl, MySQL, and the Web; a powerful system when combined.

MySQL and Perl for the Web focuses on Perl scripting combined with the MySQL database because the combination is an important one that has not been adequately documented even though it is one of the more robust systems available today. This book covers how to put a database on the web, related performance issues, form processing, searching abilities, security, common e-commerce tasks, and more.

ISBN: 0735710643
688 pages
US $49.99

Berkeley DB

Sleepycat Software

More than solely a rehash of the online documentation, this book is a tutorial on using the Berkeley DB, covering methods, architecture, data applications, memory, and configuring the APIs in Perl, Java, and Tcl, etc. The second part of the book is a reference section of the various Berkeley DB APIs.

ISBN: 0735710430
368 pages
US $45.00

Advanced Linux Programming

Code Sourcery, LLC

An in-depth guide to programming Linux from the most recognized leaders in the Open Source community, this book is the ideal reference for Linux programmers who are reasonably skilled in the C programming language and who are in need of a book that covers the Linux C library (glibc).

ISBN: 073570970X
500 pages
US $449.99

PHP Functions Essential Reference

PHP Functions Essential Reference is a simple, clear, and authoritative function reference that clarifies and expands upon PHP's existing documentation. *PHP Functions Essential Reference* will help the reader write effective code that makes full use of the rich variety of functions available in PHP.

Colophon

The Elwha River featured on the cover of this book is located in Olympic National Park—a World Heritage Site and Biosphere Reserve. The river originates on a snow finger of the park's mountainous core and flows north into the Strait of Juan de Fuca.

Historically, the Elwha was one of the largest producers of salmon and steelhead on the Olympic Peninsula. However, construction of two dams in the early 1900s prohibited fish passage to more than 70 miles of the river and its tributaries—reducing fish runs and disrupting the ecosystem.

In recent years, the river has been the focus of conservation groups. In 1992 Congress enacted the Elwha River Ecosystem and Fisheries Restoration Act of 1992, authorizing the Secretary of the Interior to buy and remove the dams and fully restore the ecosystem and native fisheries. Sadly, however, the dams remain in place today, as recently passed legislation requires cost/benefit analysis to be conducted before new environmental regulations are adopted. Environmentalists believe that removal of the dams could result in the return of nearly 400,000 salmon and steelhead within 30 years.

For more details on the Elwha River and plans for its restoration, see
`http://www.nps.gov/olym/issues/isselwha2.htm`.

This book was written primarily on Red Hat Linux using vi. It was edited in Microsoft Word and laid out in QuarkXPress. The font used for the body text is Bembo and MCPdigital. It was printed on 50# Husky Offset Smooth paper at R.R. Donnelley & Sons in Crawfordsville, Indiana. Prepress consisted of PostScript computer-to-plate technology (filmless process). The cover was printed at Moore Langen Printing in Terre Haute, Indiana, on Carolina, coated on one side.